MONTESSORI FOR EVERY FAMILY

MONTESSORI FOR EVERY FAMILY

A practical parenting guide
to living, loving, and learning

TIM SELDIN and LORNA McGRATH
THE MONTESSORI FOUNDATION

CONTENTS

Chapter 3
FAMILY LIFE THROUGH A MONTESSORI LENS

FOREWORD

Many people worldwide have heard of Montessori schools and, whether through reputation or personal experience, are impressed with the beauty, calm, and order of Montessori classes, as well as the independence, maturity, and kindness of children educated in the Montessori way.

An often-asked question is, what is the secret that allows one or two adults to manage large groups of children in an atmosphere of peace? The answer is, to a large degree, that Montessori teachers consciously learn to establish cooperative classroom communities. This book is intended to show parents how they can apply the same principles to their family's daily life.

As authors, we can barely remember a time when we weren't involved in the world of Montessori education—for us, it is a way of life. This book draws on our personal experiences as children; as parents; as Montessori guides; and as parenting coaches to many families who have sought a better way to raise their families in a spirit of kindness, respect, and partnership. Much of what we have learned came from observing and working with parents and children and from raising our own families.

Being a parent is a full-time job. In the past, moms tended to stay at home to look after children, while dads went out to work. Today, families of all shapes and sizes—whether moms and dads, same-sex couples, single-parent households, grandparents raising grandchildren, or blended families—juggle the responsibilities of work and parenting. Young children are often cared for by others, while older children spend much of the day at school and after-school activities.

" "

Children's brains are programmed to learn; stimulating them in developmentally appropriate ways is key in the early years.

At the same time, there is a growing awareness of how important the right environment and experiences are for infants, toddlers, and young children. We understand children's brains are programmed to learn, which is why stimulating them in developmentally appropriate ways is especially essential in the early years. And it never stops. As children grow, they continue to need time, attention, engagement, and support, all the way into young adulthood.

Most of us long to give our children the best home environment that we possibly can, within the limits of our time and resources. The mission that we undertake as parents is not simply to feed, cuddle, and protect our children. We also want to teach them to become independent, self-confident, successful adults who are happy and fulfilled. While that journey takes many years, it helps to have an idea of where we are heading and why we do what we do. If you are eager for a fresh perspective and some practical suggestions,

then this book is for you. We hope that it will encourage you to enjoy your time with your children more than ever. It is filled not only with practical guidance and ideas for activities to do together, but also with the message that life is meant to be celebrated. The small, everyday things that we can do to mark occasions and to reaffirm our love for one another can make all the difference, both for our children and for us as moms, dads, grandparents, or guardians.

Tim Seldin

Lorna W'Breath

Teaching our children the small ways in which they can celebrate life daily is part of creating a stimulating and harmonious home.

WHAT IS MONTESSORI?

MONTESSORI PHILOSOPHY

The term "Montessori" refers to more than 22,000 schools in more than 110 countries who follow the approach pioneered by Dr. Maria Montessori. Its philosophy involves a way of organizing classrooms and of helping children learn, as well as a way of thinking about relationships that can be applied at home, in the workplace, and beyond.

Montessori as a way of life

Most people think of Montessori as a preschool curriculum and educational approach used with very young children. While it is true that the first Montessori schools were developed with children under the age of 7, today they serve children of all ages, from the youngest up through the secondary school years. Moreover, beyond the school environment, core Montessori principles are now commonly extended into family life and businesses and used as a template for social institutions.

The Montessori way of thinking encompasses many things, but fundamentally, it is a way of creating a culture that helps people of all ages work together in peaceful, mutually supportive ways. Its approach is counter-intuitive to the more familiar one of top-down authority and control, with rewards and punishments and external

judgments about whether work is up to snuff. Montessori does encourage habits of excellence and the pursuit of carrying out tasks extremely well; however, it relies on helping children internalize values, work habits, social skills, thinking, and problem solving to achieve goals. It allows children to find or rediscover their own voice, learn to work together in ways that minimize conflict, be in touch with their true feelings, and become appropriately assertive in ways that are mutually respectful. This way of life tends to lead Montessori children to experience great satisfaction and connection with others at home; at school; and, later on, at work.

The foundation years

One of the original discoveries of Dr. Maria Montessori was that the most important time in a child's education is not the years from 12 to 18, but rather the first six years of life. When many people assumed that children were just playing—in fact, we still use the term "preschool" for centers that care for young children—she realized that, in reality, these are the years when a child's brain and nervous system develop most fully.

This development goes far beyond our normal academic concepts of math and reading skills. Children are developing foundational skills and understanding

66 99

Montessori is a way of creating a culture that helps people of all ages work together in peaceful, mutually supportive ways.

Giving children access to books and quality reference materials is a cornerstone of Montessori, helping them develop a habit of learning for life.

that will shape them for the rest of their lives. For example, they are learning about balance and coordination; executive function skills, such as organizing and planning; the first levels of independence; and vocabulary and language skills. They are also developing an inner sense of order; a sense of social norms and values; and positive attitudes about their gender, racial, ethnic, and spiritual identity. This is the time of life when children are learning how to learn.

Ideally, having an understanding of the Montessori approach before a first child is born would allow families to create, from the start, a home that supports a collaborative and cooperative culture. However, any family can begin to benefit from the insights of Montessori philosophy whenever they discover it, and families with children of all ages can learn how Montessori educators cultivate environments that are calm, peaceful, and cooperative.

" "

Montessori teaches us the art of hearing what our children are saying to us, monitoring our own thoughts, and being consistent in our responses.

Montessori encourages hands-on learning that allows children to develop practical skills and gain a deeper understanding of certain concepts.

A Montessori-inspired home

Incorporating the Montessori philosophy into the home in practical ways helps children embrace learning.

- Montessori-inspired homes recognize the value of hands-on learning. Parents understand that many of the skills and concepts children are asked to learn are abstract and that textbooks rarely bring them to life. Rather than focusing on rote drill and memory, parents offer experiences that help their children understand and use concepts.

- Families recognize the importance of books and connect children with libraries, both physical and online, to introduce them to esteemed literature and reference materials.

- Montessori-inspired homes value the importance of being outdoors as a family: gardening, discovering and caring for the natural world, hiking, and exploring.

A concept of leadership

Montessori teachers usually undergo a year or more of training to learn how to teach in the Montessori way. As part of their study, they take a course in Montessori classroom leadership, which shows them how to follow a systematic approach to establish a Montessori culture and routines to allow children choice with clear limits. These essential skills help teachers build a cooperative classroom community. This concept of leadership can be extended into the family home, with the practice of "Montessori family leadership," where strategies for developing healthy family relationships help build a special sense of community in the home.

Montessori family leadership is not about discipline in the sense of establishing ground rules and using a system of rewards and punishments to try to control behavior. Instead, it is an approach to cultivating a culture of kindness, warmth, mutual respect, and a common adherence to ways of conducting day-to-day life. It is about helping our children understand their emotions and express these in ways that are respectful and appropriate; figure out how to find their own voice without harming others; and learn that all conflict should be resolved nonviolently and to the mutual satisfaction of all parties wherever possible.

The Montessori philosophy also recognizes that each child and each family is different. What Montessori teaches is the art of hearing what our children are saying; paying attention to what is happening; monitoring our own thoughts; and following principles that tend to minimize stress, increase consistency in our responses, and enable families to build happy and harmonious homes.

Spending time together as a family, exploring and being outdoors, engenders a mutually supportive family culture.

KEY MONTESSORI PRINCIPLES

The Montessori principles set out here can be applied in the home, providing a valuable starting point for parents to help them create a family life inspired by the ethos of Montessori.

1
Be consistent

Teach children clear guidelines and reliably reinforce these by your example and leadership. When your child tests limits, be consistent and kind but firm to keep them on track.

2
Practice mutual respect

Our words and deeds should never shame. Speaking to your child with kindness and respect—picturing the adult they will become—is most likely to elicit the best in them.

3
Recognize uniqueness

Each child has their own voice and may see or respond to situations in their own way. Resist comparing children to each other or yourself. Cherish what makes a child unique.

4
Foster a sense of order

To help children think logically and follow a sequence of steps, we need our own sense of calm and order. An organized home with routines set up helps us work toward this goal.

5
Encourage rather than praise

Constantly praising children to show our approval can lead to them craving praise. By encouraging, we invite them to carry on and convey that their effort and choices are recognized.

6
Instill intrinsic motivation

When you teach correct behavior, model it consistently, and recognize and appreciate it, it tends to become second nature. Aim to instill the habit that this is the way we do things.

7
Give freedom within limits

Creating conditions where children have appropriate levels of freedom of movement and choice of activity within clear, safe limits helps develop independence and self-discipline.

8
Support lifelong learning

Ask children the right questions rather than give answers. Learning *how* to learn, understanding concepts, and thinking deeply and creatively help us navigate life.

10
Promote grace and courtesy

We help children develop grace—control of the body—and manners, its social equivalent, so they show respect and avoid hurting others, or embarrassing themselves or others.

9
Build autonomy

Part of our job is to help children master physical, intellectual, and social skills. Our goal is to raise a child who stands beside us as a young member of the community of adults.

11
Instill personal responsibility

When we take responsibility for our actions and provide an emotionally safe space where mistakes are seen as learning opportunities, we help children "own" their behavior.

MONTESSORI
FAMILY LIFE

MONTESSORI FOR ALL FAMILIES

Montessori offers a perspective on the world and promotes interpersonal relationships based on partnership. Parents who are drawn to the Montessori way come from all walks of life. Though families may have different backgrounds, those who follow the Montessori philosophy and principles, whether by sending their children to a Montessori school or by embracing Montessori in the home, tend to have much in common.

A courageous choice

It can take courage to be a Montessori parent. This is because Montessori encourages children to think for themselves and articulate their own opinions. For example, there may be moments when it would be much easier for parents of a 6-year-old if their child obediently accepted their simple explanation for why it is not practical to create a full recycling center in the middle of the kitchen. By encouraging independent thought and reasoning, Montessori challenges parents to help children explore projects and find practical solutions so that children learn how things work and what challenges a project might present.

A common outlook

The Montessori approach senses that children are capable of amazing things from a very young age. It believes that this is the case regardless of gender, race, or ethnicity. It recognizes that children from all families, regardless of social class, income, and family structure, can develop their full human potential when they are given the right stimulation and emotional support from the outset. Following Montessori principles does not mean overhauling the home or buying special learning tools. Instead, parents nurture kindness and empathy in their children and encourage the development of their innate intelligence, curiosity, creativity, and sense of wonder.

Being a Montessori family is about seeing children as unique human beings with their own personalities, interests, and emotions, no matter how young. It recognizes the importance of helping them learn to do things for themselves so they develop independence and realize their own abilities and the value of their voice in the world.

A collective aim

Montessori families believe they can help build a better world by teaching peace within the home: how to resolve conflicts without violence, hear and cherish one another, and live in a spirit of collaboration and partnership rather than shortsightedness and self-interest. Even if, initially, Montessori is discovered in search of good childcare, families who embrace Montessori come to recognize that the way to work for a better future for all is by teaching our children a way of living. When the fundamental principles resonate, Montessori is already, or will probably become, a wonderful fit for your family.

" "

With the right stimulation and emotional support from the outset, children can develop their full potential.

Montessori challenges parents to listen to children and foster a sense of curiosity in them through exploration and discovery.

FAMILY VALUES

We pass down our worldview to our children. When we raise a child, whether as biological parents, as adoptive parents, as a single parent, in a foster family, or in an extended family that includes grandparents, each of us has values we pass on.

A clear message

In Montessori-inspired homes, parents promote a set of core family values and fundamental goals. Being clear about what our values are and what we hold dear is important. However, we cannot simply impose our values on our children without displaying these values, too.

Striving to be on the same page as a co-parent and being consistent in the way we act and react on a day-to-day basis increases the likelihood that the messages that your child receives from you will be absorbed and understood and that your child will learn from the example you set.

Identifying your values

To ensure that children are clear about family values, it is helpful first to clarify the values of each adult in your family unit. Look for the values that you hold in common and identify areas where you disagree, then explore these together to see if you can reach some agreement. For example, do you share the same views regarding your child's religious education? If not, can you find a solution that works for you both? Also, how do you perceive the role of each parent? If one prefers to avoid conflict, does this leave the other parent enforcing rules?

As well as absorbing our values, children can also unconsciously absorb our biases toward or

Listening and conversing with each family member, from youngest to oldest, helps reinforce important Montessori values, such as mutual respect.

against certain areas, so it is important, too, to examine any preconceptions you have. Ideally, parents-to-be would consciously address their values in preparation for parenthood, then on an ongoing basis in their lives together to make sure that everyday words and actions continue to convey the lessons they intend to teach.

While a family's values can be determined by many factors, including ethnicity, faith, political perspective, and social attitudes, in Montessori, certain common values are aspired to, which form a solid foundation on which to build family life:

- **Families nurture curiosity**, creativity, and imagination in each other.

- **They strive to exhibit** a habit of doing things well—a passion for excellence.

- **Universal values**, such as nonviolence, honesty, kindness, empathy, and respect, are taught and shared.

- **Children are helped** to develop a global perspective and embrace differences that are the hallmark of human beings.

- **A family tradition** of service to others is encouraged.

- **Gender-based roles** are discouraged.

- **Families listen and** speak to each other with respect and thoughtfulness.

- **Conversations are** invited to discuss how each person feels if a situation arises.

- **Each person tries** to express intentions clearly and ensure actions reflect words.

- **Conflicts or concerns** are resolved directly and peacefully with the person involved, rather than harboring resentment or complaining to others.

- **Responsibilities are** shared, and each person's contribution is valued.

- **Mistakes are seen** as chances to learn.

- **Each person is treated** equitably, and families strive to address implicit bias.

FAMILY CULTURE

A family's culture is informed by its values. Families following the Montessori way develop a culture that nurtures respect, kindness, and collaboration. This may be expressed in the home environment in meeting children's emotional needs by maintaining traditions, being respectful, listening intently, and communicating thoughtfully.

An engaged child

In a Montessori-inspired family culture, children are encouraged to help with decision-making, express feelings, and try new ideas. While to some this may sound like a recipe for chaos, rebellion, and disorder, in the context of the parents being the leaders in the family and setting the tone based on their values, this is not the case. Montessori parenting aims to set limits without limiting potential, finding a balance between guiding a child and allowing for individuality and autonomy.

Challenging our perceptions

Giving children a voice can mean we may need to let go of preconceived ideas about how we think things should be and understand that we cannot mold our children like clay into the image that we have in mind. Instead, we allow them to reveal their unique personality and interests, giving them freedom within limits.

Avoiding gender-stereotyped roles can be one way to allow children to explore their own interests. For example, each person can help with the dishes, cook, or do household chores. And as children grow, helping plan the family budget and becoming involved with money matters can allow them to help with decisions.

Montessori family meetings

A key element for creating a Montessori-based family culture is a weekly family meeting where the whole family, across the generations, sits together to solve

The family meeting format

There are four parts to family meetings, as set out below. Pages 66–67 show you how to put these into practice.

- Appreciations and acknowledgments. Each person offers and receives appreciation or acknowledgment for things they have done during the week.

- Getting started. The family member facilitating the meeting guides the family through the agenda.

- What's coming up? Family members share what is coming up for them during the week so that everyone can be mutually supportive.

- Family fun! The facilitator chooses an easy, fun activity—such as a bike ride or playing a game— lasting no longer than 10 minutes to close the meeting.

How meetings take shape is governed by the age of the children. For younger families, settings remain informal and at the child's level.

problems, make agreements, learn leadership skills, think creatively, listen, share thoughts and ideas, and enjoy each other's company. By brainstorming issues, the family can explore possible solutions together. When this is done well, it fosters creative thinking, collaboration, and respect.

Family members take turns facilitating meetings, with younger members observing and learning from older ones (see p.64). Meetings provide a forum for family members to participate in honest, open communication with each other.

They are an important way for your child to express feelings, work out problems, and keep connections strong, providing a chance for them to converse on a deeper level than is the case with digital communication and even face-to-face catch-ups at meals.

Holding regular meetings, with no interruptions or distractions, gives the sense that family time together is valuable and that each person is an important part of the family. Follow the guidelines on pages 64–67 for how to hold your weekly family meetings.

A PARENTING PARTNERSHIP

Whether your parenting partner is your spouse or civil partner, your ex, a good friend, your parents, or whoever shares parenting responsibilities with you on a regular basis, it is important to have an ongoing conversation about parenting.

Starting the conversation

Being sure that you and your parenting partner are on the same page when it comes to your child's behavior and values is important in providing both consistency for your child and harmony in your adult relationship. Ideally, couples who wish to start a family would discuss child-raising practices before having a child, but most of us do not manage to do this. Instead, we have a child and then, not until we are in the middle of a situation, do we start to think about how we can best parent together or what parenting values we have in common.

To begin a conversation about parenting practices, you and your partner may want to each think about

Discussing your views together and finding common ground can help you parent consistently and thoughtfully.

❝ ❞

Talking together about your hopes and thoughts for your child as they grow leads to a strong and loving parenting partnership.

how you envision your child when they are 18 and how you can help them prepare successfully for adulthood. You might hope your child will value honesty and have empathy and courage. Or maybe you would like them to receive an education that provides them with a valuable skill set, instills confidence, and allows choice in future work. Or is their ability to be happy most important to you? You may wish that your child will grow to become a responsible adult who shows respect for others and the planet. And you may hope that they will have the confidence to express themselves.

Each try writing your thoughts down, giving yourselves enough time to really gather them together before sharing them with each other. A day or so later, share your thoughts together. See where you have similar hopes, and talk about where your views differ. Give some thought to what you can do as

parents to foster those goals as your children grow from toddlerhood to young adults.

Looking back

As you talk through these hopes, begin a discussion about what you each think about parenting; for example, what are your views on discipline? Look back and discuss how your parents handled tricky situations, such as a public meltdown, or what they did when you and your siblings argued. Are there aspects of parenting you would handle differently? Keep discussing how you both experienced family life as you grew up and return to this discussion as your child grows, asking each other how you want to resolve situations and to parent.

Even if you and your partner were brought up in similar homes with similar values and goals, you are still likely to have differences in your parenting approaches. Find out what you agree on and what you do not. Can you work out a compromise? If you have children from a previous relationship, talk to your new partner about your parenting practices. Work together to give your children as much consistency, routine, and love as possible. Brainstorming together can help you find common ground and solutions that will work for you both and other family members who care for your child.

LOOKING AFTER YOUR RELATIONSHIP

Cherishing your relationship with your partner as you experience the joys and challenges of parenting takes patience, understanding, communication, and commitment. While it is easy to see shortcomings in our partners, modeling an approach with our own behavior can be a more constructive way to build a supportive partnership and, in turn, a harmonious family home.

Listen, understand, and agree

Paying attention and listening carefully to each other is a crucial aspect of finding agreement and keeping your relationship intact. When you have a conversation, it is extremely important that you both feel that the other person is truly present and engaged.

Sometimes our partner may just need to talk and to be heard. They are not asking us to help them solve a problem or make their feelings go away. Instead, they are seeking a safe space to express their frustration, anxiety, or other feelings.

If your parenting partner is upset or wants to discuss an issue they consider to be important, make a conscious effort to stop what you are doing and focus your attention fully. Listen carefully and be sure that your partner senses that you

Spending dedicated time with your partner helps nurture your relationship and provides children with a model for a loving bond.

are truly attempting to understand. As well as listening, check whether your understanding of what they are trying to say is correct. You could say, "I think what I'm hearing you say is …," then let your partner explain if this is wrong. Listening in this way can open the door to brainstorm ideas, draw up priorities, and agree on solutions that can be applied to parenting, the whole family, and your relationship.

Acknowledge challenges

It is important to acknowledge to each other that child-rearing will be a busy, often challenging, time in the cycle of your relationship. Despite this busyness, avoid putting your relationship on hold while your children grow up, thinking that you will be able to pick it up where you left off. Focusing solely on children while they grow up, without paying attention to your adult relationship, can leave you trying to remember what you have in common with each other once your children leave home.

Taking time for yourselves as adults not only keeps your relationship intact, but also provides a model for your children in how to care for each other. Trying new things together, whether a pottery class, yoga, hiking, or woodwork, can be an excellent way to avoid getting into a rut.

Take care of yourselves

As parents, you are in a position of nurturing and supporting each of your family members. Sometimes, though, while busy taking care of others, we fail to care for ourselves. The visualization exercise above can help you take stock and assess your own needs.

Visualizing your needs

To be sure that you both have the necessary energy and calmness for parenting, take time to renew and refresh your bodies, minds, and spirits. A simple visualization can help you both think about your own needs so that you can be the best version of yourselves for your family.

Imagine a glass full of your best energy, patience, empathy, and sense of calm. Now imagine two or three empty cups and that each family member is thirsty. You fill their cups daily, so by the end of the day, your glass is empty. You are tired and need to refresh yourself to refill your parenting glass. Think of what you can do daily to achieve this, whether you read a book, go for a run, dance, sing, sit quietly to collect your thoughts, or take a bath. Find what works and make it part of your daily routine.

CHALLENGING YOUR PERCEPTIONS

As parents, we often question whether we are doing a good enough job. Self-doubt can be common, especially for first-time parents. Thinking about your own behavior and mindset is an excellent way to encourage your child's growth and learning.

Opening our minds

The real preparation for parenting is the study of ourselves. To be highly effective parents, we need to do far more than learn parenting strategies, even where these have been shown to work and have been used successfully for many years. Beyond these strategies, we need to explore our own ways of thinking about—and interacting with—our children and our parenting partner or other caregivers.

An important part of the parenting process is to ask yourself if you are ready to challenge the messages you received from your own parents. You may decide that you wish to raise your child differently from how you were raised by your parents, not necessarily as a criticism of your parents, but rather because you feel that you will improve on some of their methods. However, even with these intentions, you may sometimes catch yourself sounding like your parents and realize that you have been programmed to repeat the mindset and parenting practices that you experienced as a child.

Adapting your thinking

It is good to know that, if you do find yourself responding to your child's behavior in a way that does not feel right, you can change your thinking.

First, try to explore the ways in which you think about your child and your responses to their behavior. Some of your thought patterns may be extremely positive and effective, shaped by childhood memories of the times when

Identifying thought patterns

Here are just a few examples of conscious and unconscious thought patterns that we inherit from our own childhood. Exploring these on your own and/or with your parenting partner can help you question these perceptions.

- Children should play quietly and not interrupt adults.
- I want to be my child's best friend.
- Boys are better at math and science than girls.
- When I tell my child something, I should have to say it only once.
- I should always correct my child's mistakes.
- I should never let my child feel that they have failed.

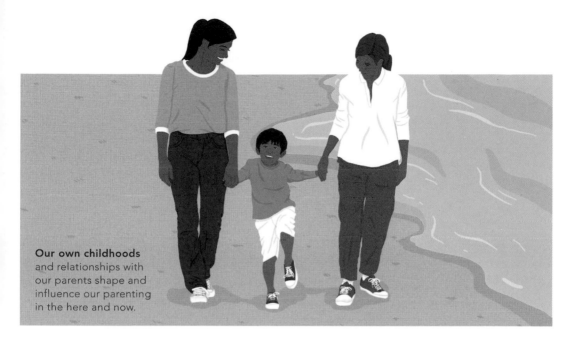

Our own childhoods and relationships with our parents shape and influence our parenting in the here and now.

your parents did an incredible job with love, kindness, and consistency. Other habits of thinking may be shaped by less positive childhood experiences and may lead you to behave negatively, interfering with your goal of creating a calm and peaceful home.

Whether habits of thinking are conscious or unconscious, they shape how you feel and how you interact. You can adapt thought patterns you are conscious of most easily. To adapt unconscious thinking, you also need to identify which thoughts shape the way you react emotionally and instinctively to your child. Once you are aware of these unconscious ways of thinking about and responding to your child and

others, you can begin to reexamine and rethink your parenting practices.

For example, you may have an ingrained thought process that girls are easier to manage than boys, or vice versa. If this is your unconscious thought process, common parenting issues that arise may confirm this bias, and raising your child may feel like a challenge. Your perception about the differences between girls and boys will influence the way that you interact with your child and color your relationship, as your child will sense your frustration and perception that they are difficult and harder to manage. Checking your bias can help you adjust your internal mindset, bringing greater harmony to your relationship.

SEEING THE WORLD THROUGH YOUR CHILD'S EYES

One of the keys to creating a calm and peaceful home is to learn how to see the world from your child's perspective. Dr. Maria Montessori challenged us to "follow the child." To do this, first we must have a sense of how children think, feel, and react.

Your child's perspective

When a young child looks up at an adult they love, from their perspective of 2 or 3 feet tall, the adult seems like a giant. To a child, the size and strength of the adult makes them seem all powerful. When children are small, this impression can make them feel overwhelmed, powerless, and without a voice.

Carrying out a simple exercise can help you appreciate the world literally from your young child's perspective. When your child is asleep, get down on the floor and observe your surroundings, or take a video of how your house looks from your child's height. The dramatically different perspective is likely to be striking.

As a parent, you are not only taller and stronger than your young child, you are also the one who meets their needs— who says "yes" or "no," pays attention, or ignores them. If we do not always understand what our children are trying to tell us, our children need to find ways to get our attention and communicate their desires by trial and error. By trying to see the world from your child's perspective, you can better understand how your child might be thinking and feeling. This can help you respond more effectively.

Your growing child

As your child grows, their thoughts and communication skills develop. Of course, each child is unique. No matter what age they are, some seem to accept their parent's guidance easily, while others may test everything their parents say or do. Your job as a parent is to listen to and try to understand your child, help them gain confidence, and find their own identity.

> **" "**
>
> Appreciating how your child sees the adults and world around them will help you understand what they are trying to communicate and respond to their needs.

Thinking about how it feels to be small can help you appreciate your child's perspective.

needs of others as well as their own, to communicate with words, and to gain skills that foster independence. They begin to realize that they have their own unique voice and that they can communicate respectfully and do things for themselves.

- **In the elementary school years**, children get better at communicating. They are increasingly interested in their peers and their relationships and preoccupied by rules and fairness, wanting to make up their own rules and try them out. They are beginning to sense their own independence and autonomy. As parents, we start to feel more comfortable and confident in their ability to make decisions and handle certain situations on their own or with a little help from adults.

- **Adolescence** sits between childhood and adulthood. One moment, teenagers act or feel like children, the next like adults. Bodies grow and change overnight. Teens want to know what their place is in the world and how they can make a difference. They become interested in sexuality—their own and others—and want to try out different ideas to discover their values and beliefs, which may or may not be the same as their parents.

- **Before your child can talk**, they cry, smile, or coo to get attention. They do not even truly recognize that they are separate beings from their primary caregivers.

- **From toddlerhood**, children gain words and are also likely to communicate their needs through tears, heart-melting smiles, tantrums, and pouting. Your young child is learning slowly to recognize the

AN EMOTIONALLY SAFE ENVIRONMENT

Just as we prepare the physical environment for our families, when we create a Montessori-inspired home, consciously preparing the emotional environment is equally crucial, ensuring that we nurture a sense of emotional safety for each member of the family.

Respecting your child

It is important that we see our children as independent human beings deserving of warmth and respect. Our children are far more sensitive to our influences than we may realize, so being careful about what we do or say in front of them is key. If you speak to the very best within your child, include them in family life, show concern for their feelings, and respect their interests, they are more likely to live up to your expectations. The following strategies will help you create a safe emotional environment for everyone in your home.

- **Create consistency and routine**. Make daily and weekly schedules that are predictable but not rigid. Children feel comfortable and secure when they have a sense of family routine. Being consistent in

Talking calmly and avoiding an angry encounter if your child arrives home later than agreed is more likely to make them reflect on their behavior and to avoid being late in the future.

your responses, too, and reacting respectfully to everyday situations creates a sense of safety, making it clear that your love is not conditional based on behavior—even if you disagree with your child's behavior, you accept and love them.

- **Set clear expectations** and boundaries positively. When children know what is expected, they are more likely to behave as we desire, within our boundaries. Convey expectations in terms of the behavior you wish to see rather than the behavior you do not. For example, if your child shouts in the home, you might say, "Please use your inside voice" rather than, "Stop shouting in the house." Describing expectations in negative terms can be heard as a command, which can trigger resentment and lead to the opposite behavior as your child tries to prove autonomy.

- **Be comfortable with mistakes**. Dr. Montessori's advice was to help children learn how to do things for themselves. Children make mistakes and can learn from them. They may forget to water the plants or to walk the dog, and older children may miss assignment dates, stay up too late, or not manage to get home at an agreed

time. When dealing with their mistakes, we hope children will learn valuable lessons rather than feel scolded. The word "discipline" means to teach and to learn (see p.40). Presenting everyday living skills allows children to practice and become more aware of how their words and actions affect others. If we protect children from mistakes that seem obvious to us, we can inhibit their independent learning process and they can be easily overwhelmed when we jump in with a quick solution.

- **Provide a "quiet" space** for thoughtful reflection (see pp.156–159). In Montessori-inspired homes, families create comfortable places where each family member can go when they are upset or disturbing the harmony of the home. This is the opposite of a "time out" space, used when parents are at a loss. Time out is usually felt as a punishment, sending a message that children are bad and need to leave. This works only as long as children dislike the experience enough to modify their behavior. A quiet space for each family member helps individuals calm themselves and consider their actions and words so that they can take responsibility, rejoin the family, and do things differently in the future.

TALKING TO YOUR CHILD

As children grow, they will hear and see things they do not understand and may want to learn more about them. While you may feel comfortable answering certain questions, there may be other topics that you find harder to discuss.

Looking at issues

Topics you may need to tackle could include:

- Questions related to current affairs.
- Anti-racism and social justice.
- Religion and moral dilemmas.
- Sexuality and gender.
- Separation and divorce.
- Illness and death.

Use these guidelines to help you navigate tricky conversations.

- **Give children** only as much information as they can absorb. The length and depth of explanations depends on a child's age and level of maturity. For example, if your 3-year-old asks where babies come from, your answer should be brief and factual. Most young children do not need to know the details from conception to birth. Your preadolescent, however, not only wants to know, but needs to know. The same applies to all "sticky" questions.

- **Be honest** with your child about your feelings. If you feel uncomfortable about a topic, express this, keeping their age and maturity level in mind. Children of all ages pick up on feelings and body language, not just words, and sense when you are not being honest about how you feel.

- **Separation and divorce** can be hard to discuss. Children can sometimes feel they are to blame. They need to know that they are not responsible and that both parents love them no matter what. The most difficult part of this conversation is explaining why you have separated while keeping the best interests of your child in mind, for example, by not blaming your coparent.

- **Different families have** different beliefs. Talk to your child about how families can hold very different views on issues such as politics, faith, ethical and moral questions, and family culture. Do clarify your family's core values, but recognize and respect other families' rights to hold their own opinions. Montessori-inspired families are likely to share many values and beliefs, but there will always be unique perspectives and traditions.

- **Be guided** by your family's core values and beliefs when answering your child's questions. If you discussed these with your parenting partner at the start of your relationship and agreed on them, this will be helpful when it comes to answering questions. When you feel secure about your values and beliefs and aligned with your parenting partner, your child is also likely to feel secure.

- **Children may be reluctant** to talk about certain topics. There may be a topic or situation you think you should discuss but sense they will find it embarrassing, uncomfortable, or upsetting and they, or you, might prefer to avoid a conversation. First, let them know that you need to talk. Ask if they are willing to talk now. If they seem distressed, it may be wise to give them time to calm down, as pursuing it when they are upset can make it hard for them to express themselves or hear what you need to say. Be clear, though, that you cannot avoid difficult conversations. You could say something like, "We do need to talk, but I can see that you are upset. Let's talk a little later when you are ready."

Finding a comfortable and relaxed place to talk about difficult-to-discuss topics can help your child listen and engage more easily.

A HOME FOR ALL AGES

In a Montessori-inspired home, parents give thought and attention to preparing an environment where all family members will feel included and at ease. There are simple things you can do to help make your home a comfortable and welcoming place for you and your family.

drawers in bedrooms and books in bookcases or on shelves, have a space for arts and crafts materials; shelves for children's toys and activities; areas for reading and study; and places to prepare food and to sit down and eat.

An inviting home

How we set up our home can promote cooperation, calmness, and a sense of routine, ensuring that where we live is a place in which each family member feels comfortable. This can be achieved whether your home is large or small and without the need to spend lots of money. With Montessori, beauty, order, and comfort all play a role.

- **Create beauty**. Ideally, your home should communicate to everyone in the family that this is a place we care about and feel comfortable in. When you walk in the door, seeing a space that is clean and neat, that has beauty and is inviting, will help each person in the family feel that they want to take care of their home and that it is a place for every one of them.

- **Think about creating order** in your home—a place for everything and everything in its place. As well as keeping clothing in closets and

Creating an orderly home, with accessible spaces for clothes and everyday objects, helps promote harmony and a sense of calm.

Clutter inhibits our ability to focus. Many families collect a lot of "stuff" for children. However, having everything out at one time can make it hard for children to focus on any one thing. Rather than a toy box or series of containers, display toys, games, and art supplies on shelves, then rotate activities and toys as your child's interests change.

- **Think about comfort**. Aim to create a home that is comfortable for everyone. When you have a baby, think about the furniture you choose and about whether you wish to have valuable or breakable objects or furniture that is not child-friendly in the house as they grow. Consider how you can create a home that is both beautiful to you as adults and which you can welcome others into, but where you do not feel anxious about things being spilled or broken by young children. Having a home that is practical as well as comfortable avoids creating arguments over dirt, spills, or marks on furniture. While you want to teach your child family ground rules, you also want to be realistic and focus on raising your child and helping them learn rather than on keeping a perfectly furnished home.

How spaces can evolve

As your children grow, your home will gradually change as they become more independent, get taller, and develop different interests and needs.

For example, you may have modified your child's bedroom when they were younger to ensure that items such as clothing were accessible for their height. As your child grows, as well as raising items to match their taller stature, your child may also want to have a say in the decor of their room and will also need dedicated areas to read, write, and work on a computer.

Planning for the whole family

An important aspect of preparing your home with everyone in mind is to consciously design spaces where your child can either help you with a task or be comfortably present while you do something else. For example, having a small table and chair in a family room or kitchen creates a space where your young child can work on a puzzle, write, or draw while you work on tasks. This lets your child know that their presence is welcome. Whether they participate in the same activity as other family members or do their own activity in their dedicated space when others are busy, they feel fully included in family life.

MISBEHAVIOR IS COMMUNICATION

We all have emotional needs. When these needs are met, we can be our best selves and are able to show compassion and empathy, to collaborate with others, to lead others benevolently, and to accomplish tasks and activities that we set out to do.

Our core emotional needs

Adults and children have the same set of core emotional needs that, when met, help us live harmoniously and productively. We need to feel loved and lovable; to have some control over our lives; to feel a sense of belonging; and to feel that we are valuable and capable.

When we feel that one or more of these needs is not being met, we might

" "

Children act out if they feel their emotional needs are not being met—to communicate that they need reassurance they are loved, valued, have some control, and belong.

take things personally, become cranky or defensive, seek attention, engage in power struggles, say and do hurtful things, or withdraw and hide.

When children behave in these ways, we call it misbehavior. Often, children do not understand exactly what they are feeling or how to ask for their needs to be met, so acting out can be their only way to let us know something is wrong. They are not misbehaving, but are unconsciously trying to communicate their need for reassurance that they are loved, that they are able to have some control, and that they are an important and useful member of their family.

The more we understand what our children are trying to tell us and meet their needs before they act out, the more likely they will be to cooperate rather than challenge; use kind words and actions rather than be mean or hurtful; to help out and be independent rather than hide away in their rooms for much of the time; and to allow you to have time with others or alone rather than constantly demand attention.

Relationship "accounts"

Thinking about your relationship with your child as a savings account that you can invest in to meet their emotional needs can help avoid perceived misbehaviors

Encouraging your child and noticing when they are doing something well helps them feel capable and builds up your relationship "account."

and cultivate and sustain harmonious family life. The things you do or say can "build up" or "draw down" this account. Responding to your child's behavior by punishing, yelling, shaming, comparing them with siblings, ignoring them, name-calling, threatening, or disempowering them by doing too much for them can all draw down your relationship with your child.

The types of behavior that build your relationship as well as meet your child's emotional needs include:

- **Being emotionally present**, listening intently, and giving your full attention.

- **Encouraging your child**.

- **Noticing** what they do right.

- **Being consistent**.

- **Making agreements** and talking about problem solving together.

Be consciously aware of how many times during the day you are "drawing down" rather than "building up" your relationship with your child. If it helps, keep a record to see if you are managing to invest more in "building up" rather than "drawing down." When you build up your relationship, observe how this affects your child's behavior.

This idea of relationship accounts applies to each relationship within the family and can likewise be used to pay particular attention to nurturing your relationship with your parenting partner.

RETHINKING DISCIPLINE

When we think of discipline, we often think of using punishment and reward to control a child's behavior. In fact, the original meaning of the word "discipline" is "to learn" or "to teach." When we see discipline as a teaching tool, we set our children up for success.

In Montessori thinking, rather than employ a system of rewards and punishments to encourage children to behave in the way we would like them to, instead we help children develop independence, inner discipline, and intrinsic motivation.

Why some methods can fail

So why does Montessori avoid the often favored use of punishment and reward? Rewards work to motivate people to behave in a certain way. Likewise, the threat of punishment tends to motivate people to avoid certain behaviors. However, both work only when someone is watching, when children believe they will be seen or caught, and depend on whether they care enough about the promised reward or the threatened punishment to modify their behavior.

In Montessori, the goal is for children to internalize their family's values and norms of behavior, whether or not other family members are present.

Fostering intrinsic motivation

Intrinsic motivation—an inner voice about who we are and how we behave— is an internal and enduring means of learning and sustaining behaviors that lead to calm and positive relationships.

When children follow and respect house rules, they develop intrinsic motivation, as they understand the importance of caring for their home and the living things within it.

All children misbehave at times. It is inevitable that they will be disagreeable or test limits when they are unsure of our expectations. However, we do not have to fight constant battles, never have a minute to ourselves, or often deal with children who are being aggressive or hurtful with their words or actions.

As parents, we can proactively teach children values and good behavior by modeling these ourselves. Meeting your child's emotional needs (see p.38) can also help minimize misbehavior. When your child's emotional needs are understood and met, they are more likely to be cooperative and able to go about their daily routines independently. See some useful strategies on pages 168–171.

Moreover, when we respond to children by being kind and firm, with the intention of helping them gain skills and understand what we expect from their behavior, family harmony is enhanced, even in challenging situations.

Setting "house rules"

Children need consistent guidelines on how and what to do at home to navigate everyday family life successfully. When clear expectations are set out by house rules (see above), which are consistently reinforced, children develop a sense of safety, security, and order.

Setting house rules

The older your child, the more detailed house rules can become. A broad, all-inclusive set of house rules might look like this:

1. In our home, we take care of all living things—plants, animals, and people.

2. We take care of the objects in our home.

Discuss together what taking care of living things and objects involves. For example, your child may question why they cannot sit on the table. You could explain that this is because it could be unsafe, could cause damage, and upsets the sense of order and is therefore non-negotiable and should be followed consistently.

House rules are the common rules of everyday life that each family member is expected to follow. Anything that involves safety, damage, or destruction should be non-negotiable. Beyond this, rules can be open for discussion. There may be certain things that adults can do and children cannot that sit outside house rules, but avoid double standards, which children may legitimately perceive as unfair and can lead to resentment.

House rules provide the framework for determining what is negotiable and what is not, in turn helping avoid frequent power struggles.

RESPONDING INSTEAD OF REACTING

It is inevitable that unpleasant, challenging, or embarrassing situations will occur between you and your child in the parenting years. When a situation arises, how you interact—whether you react or respond—will be important in shaping your relationship.

A critical moment

How you react to difficult situations with your child can make all the difference to how you build your relationship with each other and how you are able to nurture your child's independence, sense of responsibility, and growth. There are several key Montessori principles that you support when you respond to a

situation in a considered way instead of react immediately. When you respond thoughtfully, you are helping your child develop autonomy, promoting good manners—grace and courtesy—in your family, practicing mutual respect, and instilling a sense of personal responsibility. Victor Frankl, a survivor of the Holocaust, psychologist, and author, has been attributed with the quote:

Constructively working together with your child to correct a mishap can provide a valuable learning opportunity.

> **" "**
> Thinking about your responses to challenging situations with your child can help you find more positive outcomes in moments of stress.

"Between the stimulus and the response, there is a space. In that space is our power to choose our response. In our response lies our growth and our freedom."

This concept of "a space" can help us think about how we respond as parents, allowing us to envision a space between the time that something occurs between you and your child and the time when you react or respond to the situation. The space represents an important moment where you can ensure that you are responding thoughtfully instead of reacting impulsively on autopilot. Often, when we react, we make a situation worse and undermine the values that we were hoping to reinforce.

Pause for thought

Upsetting situations can develop quickly between a parent and child, often leaving little time to think through a response. You may recall instances when you have said something to your child or done something and almost instantly realized it was out of line with Montessori principles—if you already practice these—and your family values. Even if you expressed regret inwardly or out loud for reacting in this way, your child may have walked away from the situation with a sense of shame, guilt, or hurt.

By thinking about how we can reinforce family values before challenging situations arise, we become better at finding positive outcomes for our children in moments of stress.

As long as a situation is not an emergency, practicing pausing for a few seconds to center yourself can allow you to be more thoughtful in your responses. When you feel challenged, taking a few deep breaths, counting in your mind to three, or turning away for a few seconds can help you create the space where you can grow and be free to choose what your response is going to be.

A positive outcome

Thinking about how a scenario could play out, or reviewing a situation in the past, can help you consider how your response or reaction can make a difference.

For example, if a young child accidentally spills their drink at a family gathering, a parent may think they were not paying attention and react crossly, saying, "You are being clumsy, please be more careful! You stand aside and I'll clear up." The child in turn feels ashamed and embarrassed.

Alternatively, the parent could pause, then respond calmly, saying, "I'm sorry this happened. We will get it cleaned up. If you get a towel, we can clean it up together." This response helps the child become more responsible, learn a new skill, and see grace and courtesy in action.

MINIMIZING CONFLICT

Some squabbles and disagreements are inevitable in life. They may arise when a child does not want to share or take turns, when they are unhappy about doing a chore, or when they are trying to get attention. While it is not possible to avoid conflict completely (see pages 108–111 for strategies to disarm squabbles), there are steps you can take to minimize disagreements.

Identifying areas of conflict

There are many ways to prevent disagreements from arising at home. One of the best ways to avoid conflict is to have weekly family meetings (see pp.22–23 and pp.64–67) where you can discuss situations that often lead to squabbles. Here, issues that family members might disagree about, such as family chores, can be resolved peacefully.

❝ ❞

Talking through potential areas of dispute at weekly family meetings can be one of the best ways to avoid disagreements arising.

With areas such as chores (see pp.106–107), for children from 2 to 3 years up, you could agree to make a list of tasks in chart form so that names can be added as the family decides who will be responsible for each job. Add your chores to the list, too, so your child sees that you also have work to do around the house. Allowing your child to have a choice of one or more chores rather than assigning chores to them gives them a sense of ownership and choice, helping minimize conflict. You could also rotate chores weekly or monthly to avoid your child tiring of a task, keeping complaints down and interest up.

Another way to avoid or prevent conflict in the family is to ensure that everyone understands and agrees to follow the house rules (see p.41). Your agreed-upon house rules help individual family members keep on track with expectations for behavior.

Setting an example

Your goal is to help your child learn how to manage their feelings, how to listen to others as well as talk, and how to come to some kind of agreement about what will happen next. When your child observes you working out everyday challenges with others peacefully and treating others with kindness, respect, and understanding, they will learn from your example. When a disagreement does arise, your child needs to learn how to respond, how to work out differences, and how to compromise, creating a solution that works for both parties involved in the conflict.

Containing conflict

Often, parents do not know how to help children who are starting a dispute settle down and resolve conflict peacefully. They either become part of the battle, worsening the conflict, or they impose their authority, demanding that children quiet down and stop fighting, which is unhelpful for the children. If conflict starts, following the rules of engagement set out below can be helpful.

- **Your role** is to facilitate learning rather than participate in the struggle.

- **Let go of preconceived ideas** about who started it, who should know better, or what the outcome should be. Both children are responsible. Avoid judgment and strive to stay neutral.

- **Guide the children** to find their own resolution rather than solving an issue for them.

Agreeing on a family chores chart shows children that each person has a part to play and defines roles.

BEING FULLY PRESENT

Occasionally, we all need someone we love, respect, or admire—whether a partner, friend, relative, or colleague—to pay attention briefly just to us. If we do not get this attention, we may feel discouraged, disappointed, ignored, sad, determined, or unimportant.

How receiving attention helps

When we feel we have not received attention, we may try harder and even do something inappropriate to get it. Or we may give up and no longer expect to receive attention, or we may seek it from others. Children, like adults, need to be acknowledged, valued, and loved. If your child continually seeks attention, they are demonstrating that there is a greater emotional need that is not yet being met. Giving your child 100 percent of your attention for just a few moments can give them that boost, allowing them to carry on with what they were doing or need to start doing independently. Children and adults can be more autonomous when their emotional needs are met (see p.38).

There are some key elements to bear in mind when you wish to give your child your 100 percent focused attention.

- **Make sure there are no distractions**. You cannot be effective if multitasking, for example, driving the car, making dinner, texting, or looking at a screen.

- **A moment can be enough**. Just a brief moment only of your fully focused attention lets your child know that they are important and that you care.

- **Be fully present** when your child needs you to be. Children so often seem to need our attention at inconvenient moments. For example, your child may want your attention when everyone is rushing to get ready for work or school. Rather than see their behavior as annoying, consider it is an opportunity to meet their needs so that they can carry on without you. If you put other tasks on hold for a moment and attend to your child's need for attention, everyone will be happier and more productive.

When your child needs your attention

Notice signs that your child might benefit from a moment of your undivided attention:

- Is your child ignoring a request and being disruptive rather than cooperative?
- Has your child asked you a simple question?
- Is your child being particularly clingy?

" "

Giving your full
attention for just a
moment meets your
child's emotional
needs and promotes
independence.

Making eye contact, ensuring your
body language is open, and listening
fully all signal that you are giving your
child your complete attention.

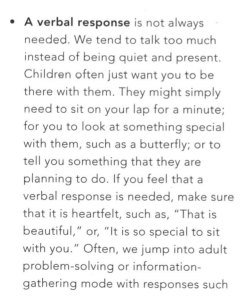

- **A verbal response** is not always
  needed. We tend to talk too much
  instead of being quiet and present.
  Children often just want you to be
  there with them. They might simply
  need to sit on your lap for a minute;
  for you to look at something special
  with them, such as a butterfly; or to
  tell you something that they are
  planning to do. If you feel that a
  verbal response is needed, make sure
  that it is heartfelt, such as, "That is
  beautiful," or, "It is so special to sit
  with you." Often, we jump into adult
  problem-solving or information-
  gathering mode with responses such

as, "Let's look up what kind of butterfly
that is," or, "I know how you can get
that done. You should ...." When
children need our focused attention,
this is a moment for emotionally
bonding with them. They are not
looking for information or solutions,
but for connection with you.

When you are fully present with your
child for a brief moment of time, you
invest in your relationship, and the
dividends are invaluable. Your child feels
loved and important and has less need
to misbehave.

ENCOURAGEMENT VS. PRAISE

We often confuse praise with encouragement. However, these are quite different and have very different results. Encouragement helps develop and support intrinsic motivation, while praise does the opposite.

How praise affects us

Praise tends to promote dependence on the approval of others. It is a type of external reward, as opposed to the intrinsic motivation that comes from encouragement. When children engage in everyday activities such as painting a picture, cleaning their room, raking leaves, or achieving a good grade on a test, parents can either encourage or praise them. When we immediately tell our children how much we love what they have done, how proud it makes us feel, and how much we want them to do it again, we may do so innocently. Our intention is not to turn the focus onto ourselves; however, this quick praise tends to make children dependent on our approval. If we say "Good work!" or "I love that!" time and again, our words

> **" "**
>
> Children experience a sense of self-satisfaction and pride when encouraged, which helps them grow in confidence.

Though your child may not carry out a job to your standards, they are learning to take pride in performing a task.

tend to become meaningless, and children can become "praise junkies." Breaking the cycle of meaningless praise is incredibly beneficial for children.

Praise involves judgment, approval from others, focus on outcome, and competition. It does not give a child any usable feedback for future activities. If, at your annual work review, your employer gave you a list of five areas of your job and for each made comments such as "fine job," "excellent work," and "good reviews," you might feel pleased but would not have any useful information to help you grow professionally.

The power of encouragement

An encouraging review might include an employer also suggesting you think about how to develop organizational or leadership skills, strategies, and ways to meet goals in a timely manner or to be a self-starter. Likewise, if you ask questions that help your child reflect on what they have done and how they feel, they are able to experience self-satisfaction and a sense of accomplishment. Their confidence will grow and they will be more likely to try new things and learn for the sake of learning, encouraged by their own sense of pride. Encouragement is based on acceptance, process, learning, gaining skills, and pleasure.

The art of encouragement

Children gain so many benefits when we encourage rather than praise. They can see themselves as contributing members of their families, schools, and communities.

- Point out how much work they put into a project, their focus on detail, and their concentration and perseverance.
- Ask what your child liked best about a process, what media worked best for them, how they felt when they completed it, and how it helped others.

Focusing on the process

An important observation is that from birth to about 6 years of age, children are in a developmental stage where the process is more important than the outcome. They do things out of interest and enjoyment in an activity and, usually, are not concerned with the final result. For example, a young child helping sort clean laundry focuses on getting it out of the machine or off the dryer, helping carry the laundry basket to the place where it will be folded, then sorting and folding items. Whether or not socks are matched or towels folded as you would wish is not important to them. For a young child, the sense of achievement comes from the process of getting the laundry from dryer to drawer.

HELPING YOUR CHILD BE INDEPENDENT

One of our goals as parents is to help our children develop a sense of independence and autonomy while also understanding that we are all, at the same time, interdependent. We teach this to our children step by step as they grow from early childhood to adulthood.

Being your child's mentor

The ways in which we respond to our children when they feel as if they need assistance can lead them either to feel self-confident and capable or that they are dependent on others. We should be their mentors and trusted guides rather than their "fixers." Our responses are meant to help them become emotionally strong and resilient.

" "

Maria Montessori said that if young children had the right words, they would ask us, 'Help me learn how to do this for myself.'

Your child starts to learn from the day they are born. Everything is a first-time experience. Most of us are aware of this when our children are infants. However, once children take their first steps, it can be easy for parents to forget that they are constantly teaching their children what to do and how to be. As your child grows, they will continue to learn everyday skills from you, from how to wash their hands and face as a toddler to managing an allowance when older. Sometimes you will teach your child lessons intentionally, while at other times your child learns simply by watching you. Each time you teach a skill or help them gain understanding, they become more capable and confident.

Guiding your child

You are your child's first and most influential teacher. The best teachers ask questions that help children think about a situation and plan their next step rather than give all the answers or solutions or do things for them. The aim is to empower children to be independent.

There may be times when your child says, "Nobody will play with me at school," "I can't do this science project," "I fell and scraped my knee; it hurts," or "I wanted to wear this outfit today and it's in the laundry." Take a

Working side by side lets your child observe how you carry out a task.

moment to center yourself before responding so that you can give support and guidance, if needed. First, acknowledge their feelings. Then respond with caring questions that will help them develop relationships, complete assignments, take care of themselves, accomplish tasks, and solve problems. When your child reaches out to you and your response is to guide them lovingly, they learn that they are capable and that it is okay to ask for help when needed.

Follow a few basic principles when you want to teach your child to do something correctly, whether tying shoelaces or helping wash the dishes:

- **Be very thoughtful** about the steps they need to follow to accomplish the task correctly.

- **Show them how** to do the task slowly and carefully, step by step, inviting them to try it for themselves.

- **Try to be silent** while showing them how to do something, saving words until the end of the task. Demonstrate a skill slowly and carefully so your child can watch what you do, then try it, too. Expect mistakes at first. Each mistake provides an opportunity to learn, whether that is how to do a task correctly or, for example, how to clean up an accidental mess.

FAMILY LIFE THROUGH A MONTESSORI LENS

A STIMULATING HOME ENVIRONMENT

Just as Montessori classrooms are designed with the children who learn there in mind, you can create a Montessori-inspired home environment for each family member.

Montessori classrooms deliberately create an environment that promotes a sense of order, independence, comfort, intellectual stimulation and engagement, and love of learning for all members of the classroom community, no matter what age, interests, or skill level. This is referred to as a "Montessori-prepared environment." Likewise, you can build a Montessori-prepared home environment with some simple steps, taking into account the ages, interests, and skills of each member of your family.

" "

An organized, aesthetically appealing environment that reflects your family's interests is key to creating a stimulating family home for all.

THE KEY PRINCIPLES

Following three basic principles will help you plan, prepare, and enjoy a family home that embraces Montessori's approach.

Whether your home is small or spacious, ensuring that it is well organized, making it aesthetically appealing, and reflecting your interests in your home environment will all create a home that reflects Montessori values and principles.

Have a place for everything

Organizing your home so that items are stored methodically and can be easily found, systems are maintained, and your environment is free of clutter creates a sense of order with everything in its set place. When your child can access items from a young age, this facilitates their ability to be increasingly independent by learning practical skills that allow them to participate in all aspects of family life.

Create aesthetic appeal

Try to create a home that feels warm, inviting, clean, and comfortable for each family member and for guests. Of course, what appeals to your child may not appeal to you. This can be reflected in their own space, for example, by painting their room a color they love or by referencing a part of contemporary culture or history they are fascinated by in the decor.

Reflect your interests

Fill your home with stimulating items such as books, art, music, and things to do and learn that reflect and support each family member's interests. Include skills and interests of your own that you would like to introduce to your child. Elements might be as varied as celebrations and symbols of your faith or traditions, a nature corner, a workout area, a library collection, pets, a telescope, a creative projects area, or a place to listen to music. Create a home where exploring and developing ideas and interests together is a family goal.

Ensuring that items in your home are organized instills the idea that everything has a dedicated place.

THE BEDROOM

Your child's bedroom is their personal space. Even if sharing with a sibling, children have a special attachment to their room. Help your child create and maintain a room that conveys warmth, comfort, safety, and order and reflects their personality and changing interests.

An emerging identity

When your child is an infant or toddler, you decide on furnishings, toys, and clothing. By the age of 3, your child may have their own ideas and can begin to have a say in how their room is arranged. At first, involve them just a little. For example, you may choose an elephant picture and have two places in mind for it. Offer them a choice: "Do you want the elephant near your closet or your bed?" The older the child, the more collaborative the process; eventually, your child will do most of the planning.

Allowing your child to help plan and design their room fosters independence, creative thinking, problem solving, and a sense of order. Creating a room for and with them will result in one that they are excited about, comfortable in, and love.

What to consider

Use these guidelines for a Montessori-inspired bedroom for all ages.

- **Decide on house rules**. Follow your family values to decide on some basic rules for what your child can bring into their room. For example, can food be eaten there? Can computers, phones, screens, and video games or pets be allowed at any time?

- **Hang items at your child's eye level**. Get down to their height to see where to put photos, bulletin boards, and art.

- **Help your child create order**. Display toys and belongings in a visually appealing way. Using containers or toy boxes to store items may feel like an easy way to keep your child's room tidy; however, children can be overwhelmed when faced with too many things thrown together in a disorderly way. When each item has a set place, you help your child experience a sense of order. With practice and consistency, your child will develop a habit of putting items back in their designated place. Instead of using large containers or overcrowding shelves, display just 8 to 12 items on accessible shelves when your child is young to instill this habit. If they tire of an activity, put it away for a while and bring out something else to ignite new interest.

- **Make clothing accessible** for young children. Lower closet rails and use the bottom drawer of dressers for their clothes. This appeals to their sense of order, and when they can start to dress themselves, at around 18 months, helps them do this independently.

- **Choose furniture** for your child's size and needs. Whether a first bed, a mattress on the floor, or a bunk bed, try to ensure that your child has a place to sleep that is comfortable, safe, and allows them independence. If there is space, a child-sized table and chair are a welcome addition to a child's room.

- **Make room for books**. With Montessori, books are revered and considered precious. They are usually found in every room of the house. Have a dedicated space for books in your child's room to help them learn to treat books with care and respect.

- **Think about lighting**. Nothing is better than natural daylight, but consider the artificial lighting in your child's room, too. It is important for their room to be well lit, with various sources of light that will allow them to read, write, draw, and do other activities without straining their eyes.

Arrange your child's room to suit their perspective—making sure that activities are within reach and wall hangings are placed at their eye level.

Ages and stages

18 months–6 years
Do not overwhelm your child with too many toys. Choose fewer toys that are durable, beautiful, and made from natural materials rather than lots of plastic and battery-run toys.

6–12 years
During this stage, a desk, reading lamp, and chair give your child a space to study. Limit the use of digital devices in bedrooms.

12–18 years
Allow your adolescent child to do most of the planning and arranging in their bedroom, with your consent and advice.

THE KITCHEN

The kitchen is often the hub of family life, a place where family members gather to prepare food, to talk, and to be close to one another. Young children in particular enjoy helping out in the kitchen and spending time with parents while they work there.

you create a sense of order that helps your child navigate the kitchen calmly and confidently. Working together to prepare meals and clean up not only helps your child develop useful life skills, but also creates a family community. For young children, simple adjustments make it easy for them to help out.

An accessible space

Organize the kitchen to assist and encourage your child to develop the everyday skills that allow them to be helpful and become independent. When everything has a place and is accessible,

- **Set aside a low refrigerator shelf** to store prepared drinks or a small pitcher of water, fruit, and ingredients for sandwiches and snacks. Allowing your child to help themselves to a snack or drink teaches them self-regulation.

Ages and stages

18 months–6 years
Place items in reach so even very young children can help prep, independently get food for themselves, and clean up. As impulse control and coordination grow, use child-sized ceramic plates, glasses, and metal cutlery. (Use a butter knife until about the age of 4.)

6–12 years
Your child can help with simple cooking tasks. Teach them about basic nutrition, cleaning surfaces and utensils, and safe food storage.

12–18 years
Teens can help with meal planning, grocery shopping, cooking, and cleaning up.

Easily accessible plates, cups, bowls, and eating utensils encourage independence in your young child.

" " OUR STORY

Throughout the stages of Otis's life so far, we have made a point to set up the spaces in the house so that they are functional and accessible for a 3-foot person, allowing him to be engaged and safe.

He has his own cupboard in the kitchen with his plates and utensils so that he can access them when he is getting lunch or a snack. He also has a step stool in the kitchen so that he can reach the counter and help prepare some of his food. He especially likes to help us with cookies, cakes, and bread—bread-making is his favorite! He has some experience with this culinary art, as he has baked bread at school. He is so proud when he shows us how to knead the dough. By giving him ownership and providing a right-sized kitchen environment, he has freedom to organize things how he likes them while at the same time keeping items safe and tidy.

Brendan and Ann Marie, parents of Otis, aged 4 years

- **Use nonbreakable containers** for peanut butter, jams, and spreads so your child can successfully get out and put away ingredients while they are working on holding and carrying skills.

- **If space allows**, a child-sized table and chair allows young children to set up and eat their food independently.

- **Put plates, cups**, and napkins in a low cupboard or on a low shelf. Store cutlery in a low drawer or basket. Ideally, use child-sized metal cutlery (see box, opposite), either custom-made or smaller items from your set. Using unbreakable plates and cups until 3 to 4 years of age helps children gain skills confidently and safely.

Prepping and clearing up

A sturdy stool or a set of small, stable steps allows a young child to help wash up or prep food at a counter. Show your child how to wipe the counter after use to instill this habit for life. A child-sized broom, dustpan and brush, and mop will mean that, from a young age, your child can help clean the kitchen floor.

EATING AREAS

Whether you have a separate dining room or meals are shared around the kitchen table, aim to make your mealtimes a pleasant experience for everyone (see pp.78–81). Encourage children to help in both setting the table and cleaning up after a meal.

Setting the table

Getting your child involved regularly in setting the table for the family or guests provides an invaluable lesson in everyday living skills. Making the table look inviting and orderly emphasizes that mealtimes are valued moments for all.

House rules for family meals

Meals are a time to be together, enjoy your food, and talk about your day (see pp.78–81). House rules, such as the ones below, can make mealtimes enjoyable and harmonious.

- Set a rule that digital devices, television, or loud music are not allowed at meals so you avoid these distractions.
- Consider how long children should stay at the table. For example, if parents and/or older children are engaged in conversations that a younger child finds uninteresting, may they ask to be excused, or should they wait until everyone has finished eating or they are excused by an adult?
- Agree that everyone helps clean up: clearing plates; putting waste in a trash can or a recycle bin; and washing or scraping or rinsing dishes, then loading the dishwasher.

If you use a tablecloth, encourage your child to help with this. They can carry it to the table, unfold it and arrange it, and put soiled cloths in the laundry. Your younger child will most likely need help placing a tablecloth, even on a small table. Placemats, used with or without a cloth, can be easier for a young child to arrange, and these also help create a feeling of order.

Montessori encourages using cloth napkins to model the principle of reusing items rather than disposing of paper napkins. Your child can also learn the skill of folding or rolling them, how to use them, and how to launder them.

As soon as your child develops sufficient coordination and shows interest, they can help carry plates to the table, setting one on each placemat or on the cloth in front of each chair. They can also collect and bring cutlery to the table. Show them how to carry knives, forks, and spoons safely and place them correctly.

" "

Involving your child in preparing the table for a meal and clearing up afterward helps them feel that they have an important role to play.

Think about the eating experience from your child's perspective. For example, are dishes and pitchers light enough for them to lift and manage?

Ages and stages

18 months–6 years
Your toddler can carry cutlery and napkins in a basket to the table for you or an older sibling to set out. From around the age of three, as strength and coordination develop, they can help set up and clean the table.

6–12 years
Your child can start to handle more delicate dishes and place glasses at each setting now, and help wash dishes or load the dishwasher.

12–18 years
Teens can engage in the entire mealtime process. They can also model grace and courtesy for younger siblings.

Your child may need help carrying pitchers of water or drinks to the table. Think of ways to make this task possible, even for younger children. For example, you could carry a large pitcher of water and your young child could carry a smaller, child-sized pitcher.

Learning table manners
The dinner table provides a perfect opportunity to model and teach grace and courtesy on a daily basis. Family members practice and use manners when interacting, and they move carefully and thoughtfully when setting the table, passing food, pouring drinks, and cleaning up when the meal is done.

Like any lesson you teach your child, teaching table manners involves first modeling the behavior you are looking for in them. Give short, simple lessons on the right way to do things, such as eating soup with a spoon, cutting food, or asking politely and responding with "thank you."

If your child drops or spills something, treat it as a chance to teach them how to clean up. If they forget to ask politely or say "thank you," respectfully remind them how to ask so that they are not embarrassed or pushed into a power struggle.

FAMILY ROOMS AND PLAYROOMS

A family or play area—whether your home's living room, a separate room, or a designated space in a room—provides an informal area where families can gather together to play with toys, watch television, play video or board games, or enjoy other similar activities. This shared space promotes and enhances your family community.

Keep things in order

As with other rooms in your home, try to create and maintain order in this informal area. All too quickly, toys can end up scattered from one end of the room to the other, becoming an obstacle underfoot and a challenge to put away. Consider the following when organizing the family room.

- **Think about how** family members typically like to use this space. For example, does your family love to watch television together or enjoy playing multiperson video games? Or do you use the family room as a place to read quietly or as a space where toys are played with and stored? Consider the space you have available, what your family's focus will be for most of the time, and what sort of furniture will work best in this family space.

- **Find ways to arrange toys**, games, craft materials, or other items you wish to keep here neatly in the available space. Shelves or wall hooks can store items in an orderly way, while a sturdy basket or storage bin can hold bulkier items such as building blocks and construction materials. Do what makes sense in the space that you have. Organizing in this way helps each family member follow the principle that everything has its own place where it is kept when not in use.

Ages and stages

18 months–6 years
Be sure your child can reach books and play items safely. Place anything that can be easily broken or pulled down out of reach.

6–12 years
Continue to teach your child to be mindful of others in the common space, putting away items after use, asking others if the television will disturb them, and sharing with siblings.

12–18 years
Work out house rules around impromptu visits from friends to assess when they use the shared family space or their bedroom.

With a little planning, family rooms and playrooms can be organized so that family members can enjoy activities side by side, in a harmonious manner.

- **Establish a rule** that family members can take out just one or two things at any one time so others in the family can move around safely. A rolled mat or rug in the room that your child can take out and spread on the floor to define their play area can be helpful, giving them a dedicated space, for example, to construct items with building or interlocking blocks or to work on a floor puzzle. Depending on your child's and family's interests and the space, you may also want to have a table and chairs where children and others can sit to work on puzzles or nonmessy craft projects.

- **Are any activities not allowed here**? For example, do you want to avoid energetic games, such as tag or play wrestling, and are snacks allowed?

- **Bear in mind** that some house rules, such as taking good care of things, not playing music too loudly, and not leaving leftover food in a room, apply to all areas of the house because they involve being considerate of others and keeping each other safe.

EVERYDAY STRATEGIES
FAMILY MEETINGS

The concept of the family meeting, introduced on pages 22–23, is one of the most important Montessori strategies for creating an atmosphere of inclusion in your family. In family meetings, each person is included and has a voice at the table.

The lessons learned at weekly family meetings are invaluable during your child's years at home with you. They will continue to use the skills they learned at these meetings when they start their own family and in their work life and community life.

Meetings are facilitated by family members on a rotating basis, with each person having an opportunity to lead. The role of facilitator may come more naturally to some who have had plenty of experience in meetings, while others are learning this valuable life skill. By starting with the oldest, children can observe and prepare for this role—children as young as 4, with help from an older family member, can begin to facilitate. By rotating leadership, each person has the chance to be empowered as a leader and supported in learning this new skill.

Meetings normally run for 20–30 minutes, including a closing fun activity. If an issue is not resolved in this time frame, it can be carried over to the following week. They should follow a set format for consistency, as outlined on pages 66–67.

" "

Family meetings, where each person is given a turn to express their feelings and ideas, promote open communication.

" " **OUR STORY**

When our oldest child, Cooper, was about 5 years old and our daughter, Madeline, was 2 years old, we took a parenting class because we were starting to question whether we were on the right track for Montessori kids. One of the most valuable practices that we learned was the importance of a weekly family meeting.

We began to have our meetings right away. We hadn't realized how much a toddler takes in from family conversations, even when we thought she was just playing with her toys. Each child in their own time became a good facilitator, leader, and creative problem solver. They were also empathetic and appreciative of each other and us.

We also noticed that as time went by and our children got close to the end of their elementary school years, our meetings changed a bit. They became less regular and more casual than when the children were younger. Everyone had busy schedules, but when one of us had something to discuss as a family, we would all make time to chat and figure things out together.

One of my most cherished parts of a meeting is the time for acknowledgments and appreciations. The children always remind us if we forget to include that time, even when we are all very busy.

Jon and Sophie, parents of Cooper, age 18, and Madeline, age 15

FAMILY MEETINGS IN PRACTICE

1
Starting the family meeting

Weekly family meetings, ideally at a set time, begin with appreciations or acknowledgments. This gives children and parents a moment to express positivity about being together and is a chance to look at each person's growth and contributions. The facilitator starts, choosing a family member and thanking them for one thing they did or helped with during the week, then other family members follow.

2
Discussing issues

During the week, family members add items for discussion to a blank agenda. At the meeting, the facilitator runs through them. When an item is raised, everyone brainstorms, so children learn to be part of a team that problem-solves without blame or shame. The meeting leader gains skills in helping others be creative, be thoughtful, and stay on task. They may also decide to postpone an item until the next week.

3
What is coming up?

Each person shares their activities or obligations for the coming week; for example, a child may have a dance performance one evening, and a parent a work presentation one day. Sharing what will be happening in the coming week gives everyone a sense of what to expect and means they can support and help each other. Children learn to be sensitive to others' needs, concerns, challenges, and activities.

4
Finishing up

After spending 15–20 minutes in discussion, the last 10 minutes or so of the meeting are spent enjoying a family activity chosen by the facilitator. Ideally, activities involve all family members and are interactive, such as a game or a short walk, rather than passive or screen-based. Ending in this way gives everyone a boost and ensures that each family member leaves on a positive note.

" "

Taking part in family meetings
shows children how to problem-
solve with others.

All members of
the family—including
visiting grandparents
and relatives—take part
in family meetings.

MESSY SPACES

Hobbies, interests, and activities can be messy, and items for projects may need to be left in place so that they can be returned to on another day. Allocating a "messy space" in your home allows family members to pursue interests without creating chaos.

Ordered "messy" spaces

Finding a space where your child can pursue messy activities fosters creativity. Younger children are also likely to want to be around you as much as possible, so when planning a messy space, think about the activities that each family member enjoys and consider whether these can be done in the same space.

Ages and stages

18 months–6 years
Lay down a heavy plastic covering on the floor in part of a room or put a washable cover on a child-sized table. Place paints, brushes, clay, or other supplies on a small shelf or designated area of a shelf. You might wish to purchase a child-sized easel. Be present when your child is working in this area to guide them and ensure safety.

6–12 years
Provide advanced arts and crafts materials and tools in line with interests and skills. As your child gets older, they can work without constant supervision.

12–18 years
Evolve this space to reflect more focused interests as your child gets older.

Providing your child with an area to enjoy messy activities allows them to engage freely in creative pursuits.

" " OUR STORY

I started noticing that my son's backpack was full of what I considered trash—broken rubber bands, the inner ring from a roll of tape, and bits of string. I asked him what they were for, and he just said that he needed them. I cleared out any insect-attracting items such as broken crackers and left the rest for whatever it was he had in mind. Then I noticed items moving from the recycling bin to his bedroom: egg boxes, milk cartons, cardboard boxes of various sizes.

He said that he needed them all. So we agreed that he would keep them in a designated "messy" area in his room,

then I took a deep breath and went with it. One day, he emerged with a "smoothie shop" made out of the cardboard and trash, each part thoughtfully glued together. With grace and courtesy, he took our orders and we played along. He was so proud, and I silently thanked his Montessori teachers for showing us how to let him follow his interests.

Tara, mother of John, aged 7 years

As with other areas, keep order in mind when planning a messy space so that utensils for activities are easily located and items are unlikely to be knocked over. Clutter and disorder compromise safety and make it harder to concentrate on the project at hand.

Being creative with space

If you do not have a spare room to turn into a messy space, think about how to provide a creative area for your child in a bedroom, kitchen, or living room (see Ages and Stages, opposite). Your child's needs will vary depending on their age and interests, but the basic concept remains the same: your child feels they have the freedom to explore hobbies and interests while you maintain order and avoid a mess. By providing a controlled environment for your child to create, construct, and explore at home, you encourage creative thinking and self-expression.

OUTDOOR SPACES

Montessori teaches children that they are part of the natural world and that all living things are interdependent. Think about how to use outdoor environments to teach your child about nature, support their development, and enjoy family time.

Spending time outdoors

Most children love to be outdoors, to wander around and explore, to climb trees, to look at flowers and berries, and possibly to play with a family pet. Many children also enjoy working in a garden or outside space and, when given the opportunity, feeding small animals such as rabbits, ducks, and chickens.

Whether you live in an apartment without a garden, have a small outside space, or have an area big enough for some play equipment, finding ways to give your child the opportunity to play and learn outdoors is invaluable.

A stimulating space

Depending on your child's age, family interests, and space, as well as your local climate, consider the following when planning how to enjoy outdoor environments with your child:

- **Whether in your garden or a park**, find areas for your child to run and play. As well as providing the exhilarating opportunity to run, this helps them gain dexterity, agility, and muscle tone. Where possible, using equipment such as a child-sized basketball hoop or a sports net can also be stimulating.

- **Think about outdoor activities** that feed your child's imagination. This

Ages and stages

18 months–6 years
Draw your child's attention to plants, trees, seeds, berries, and small animals, helping them recognize and name them.

6–12 years
Work as a family to keep your environment tidy: rake leaves, pick up twigs, and trim bushes. By 12, your child might help mow the lawn.

12–18 years
Let your teen develop gardening interests, for example, by growing herbs from seed.

" "

Giving your child the chance to play and learn outdoors is an invaluable way to support their development and teach them about the natural world.

Spending time outdoors with your child gives you an opportunity to introduce them to the cycles of nature and to teach them to respect their environment.

could be a simple sandpit or swing or, if space allows, climbing equipment, a playhouse, or even a basic treehouse.

- **If there is space**, an outdoor table allows you to eat meals together in the open or to enjoy activities such as reading and drawing outside.

- **Plan a shady area** to offer protection from the sun.

- **Think about creating** a family garden to plant and grow flowers and vegetables (see p.112). This could be in a small garden plot, in a container, or in a window box.

- **Find out about** local parks, hiking trails, or community gardens that you can enjoy as a family.

- **For a more ambitious project**, if you have space, you might consider building a home for a few small farm animals to care for. Alternatively, enjoy a trip to a small petting zoo.

Stewards of the earth

Sharing the world of nature with your child—whether when on a nature hunt in your garden, hiking on a countryside trail, or growing herbs on a windowsill— teaches them that we are all connected to nature and dependent on It. From the start of their life, spending time with your child outdoors helps them appreciate the relationship between living things and the environment.

- Being outside helps them learn that each plant and animal is affected by the climate, soil, and geographical features of its environment, as well as by the other plants and animals that live there, each one striving to feed, grow, and reproduce. Your child will develop an attitude of stewardship toward the earth—caring for wild areas, as well as pockets of nature in the city or suburb.

- Teach your child to treat living things with care. Explain that you should gather flowers for a set purpose only and not overpick a plant. Fresh wildflowers can be dried, pressed, or put in a vase to preserve them for as long as possible. Encourage them to study flowers, comparing species and counting petals and stamens. As the weather changes, they can look for nuts, fruits, and berries, noticing how these are distributed and which animals forage them.

DAILY ROUTINES

One of the defining concepts of a Montessori-inspired home is to prepare an environment where children can learn to be independent, self-disciplined, and organized each day.

This is a very different philosophy from permissive parenting, where children have no limits on their behavior or the choices they make. It also differs from families where the parents make the rules and the children are expected to follow routines and decisions made for them. The Montessori approach is authoritative—firm at the edges, warm and empathetic at heart. The goal is to teach children to recognize that their voice matters. They can do things for themselves, learning how to be increasingly masterful and independent, while at the same time understanding that with freedom comes responsibility. In this section, we explore the daily structures and routines that will help your child develop and thrive.

" "

Building routines into certain parts of your day can help children feel supported by a structure and teaches them to be independent.

A FLEXIBLE FRAMEWORK

Children tend to respond best when there is just the right amount of structure and routine in their daily lives—not too much and not too little, a sort of "Goldilocks" approach.

The main areas where routines help families are when getting up and ready in the morning and during mealtimes and bedtime. How you structure your family's free time and manage screen time are also key.

Routines involve thinking about a daily sequence of steps that can be helpful when followed in a particular situation. While the sequence does not need to be rigid, your child should feel supported by a structure, which in turn reduces stress and squabbles.

Times of transition

There are times when children need to transition from one activity or part of the day to another—for example, moving from breakfast to play time or transitioning from school to extracurricular activities. As you guide your child, you can work out if they need help to transition or manage this easily. Be aware of their personality and needs. Is a gentle reminder enough, or do they need concrete support to transition? If so, certain tactics can be helpful.

- **Consider setting a kitchen timer**, say, for 10 minutes, to focus your child on tasks such as getting dressed and ready for breakfast.

- **A calming strategy** can help your child transition from playing outside to coming in for dinner. For example, invite them to sit on the doorstep to have a drink of water and catch their breath before coming in. Remind them what you need to do together to get the table ready or prep food.

- **Some children respond well** to a checklist. This could be written or made up of simple illustrations that represent actions, such as getting out of bed or brushing their teeth.

A visual checklist of what needs to be done at certain times of the day can be a useful tool for some children.

GETTING READY FOR THE DAY: YOUNG CHILDREN

From 18 months to 6 years, children need direction and structure in their day. At the same time, Montessori encourages us to "follow the child." Aim to balance your child's need for structure and routine with the recognition that each child is unique.

Setting the tone

Montessori said that adults need to prepare themselves so that they can set the tone for the day with their calm, quiet presence. Following a routine whereby you wake early to enjoy a jog, listen to quiet music while thinking about the day ahead, or read a chapter of an enjoyable book ensures a more relaxed start to the day, in turn helping your young child feel calm and reassured.

A smooth start

Consistency and routine are essential for young children to develop trust and feel assured that their needs will be met. However, plans should not be rigid and must be designed with the individual child in mind. Here are some ideas to consider for the start of the day.

- **Prepare clothing choices** and lunches with your child the night before. You can also set up the table for breakfast

Setting out clothes the night before is a simple task that saves valuable time during busy mornings.

and encourage 3- to 5-year-olds to begin to serve themselves in the morning. If your child takes a packed lunch to school, they may enjoy helping make this so that they can have a say on what goes in their lunchbox. Offer healthy choices. By being part of this process, they are learning to select food from different food groups and to balance their diet. They are also more likely to eat food when they have been involved in the decision-making. Invite your toddler to help make snacks on weekends to prepare them for this task.

- **Develop a list of tasks**—whether a mental list or a written one—that need to be done at the start of the day. Include every task—whether big or small—from feeding and dressing your baby, to supervising older children while they have breakfast, to eating your own breakfast. Then work out at a family meeting who is responsible for each task. A regular set of morning tasks helps young children develop habits and a rhythm. Some children fall easily into a pattern, while others may need a chart, which could be in the form of illustrations, to keep them on track.

- **Give yourself and your child** plenty of time to get ready in the morning to allow for plans going awry, such as a cup of juice being spilled, a dog walking slowly, or a toddler who does not get to their potty in time.

66 99 OUR STORY

After he had gotten dressed, I saw my son shuffling, as children do when they need their potty. I asked if he needed to use his potty and he replied, "No." As we got ready to leave the house, his feet started to shuffle faster. "Are you sure?" Again, he said, "No."

His shuffling became more urgent. I said, "I think you need to go" and lifted him to carry him to the potty. I felt a warm trickle against my hip and knew that I had invited myself to experience the consequences of waiting too long. With my toddler, I had to remove soiled clothes, put them in the laundry, and find new clothes. The lesson I was trying to instill in him I had to practice, too. In my rush, I was trying to avoid the unavoidable. He might have made it to the potty if I had stopped and said at the start, "Let's go ahead and try."

Alicia (@montessibaby @teachlearnmontessori), mom of Charlie, aged 2

GETTING READY FOR THE DAY: OLDER CHILDREN

From the age of 6 up through the adolescent years, your child becomes increasingly able to take on more responsibilities, organize their time, and put the family values that they learned from you in their early years into practice.

Tools for life

Your child practices using the skills, knowledge, and beliefs they have acquired as they navigate each day. As they use these tools, inevitably making some mistakes along the way, they are preparing themselves to be on their own and independent one day. Creating routines from the start, when your child is very young, can minimize stress and helps your child feel capable.

Bear in mind that 6- to 7-year-olds and 10- to 12-year-olds are beginning new stages of development. As children enter a new stage, they sometimes seem to have lost or forgotten much of what they learned earlier. They may seem easily distracted, clumsy, and very disorganized. As their bodies and minds change, this can be confusing and disrupt their usual sense of order and routine. Doing as much preparation as you can the night before makes morning routines easier to follow and gives you time to deal with any hiccups patiently.

A start-the-day plan

Just as when your child was younger, think about what needs to be done to prepare for the day and make plans so everyone can get off to a good start.

- **In the evenings**, encourage your child to put homework and books into their backpacks as they complete a piece of work or when family study time is over so these are packed for the morning. If your child takes a

A moment of complete focus

Busy mornings can make it hard to give your complete attention to your child. If your child asks you to look at something that interests them while you are getting ready in the morning, you may be tempted to put them off. As a result, they may feel brushed aside and be less cooperative.

A different outcome
Now, imagine stopping for a few minutes and focusing totally on the thing that caught their attention, sharing their wonder or interest. Your child's needs will have been met, and what might have escalated into a time-consuming, energy-sapping situation instead becomes a special moment. Everyone is able to get back on task and feel good about themselves and each other.

packed lunch to school, they can prepare this the night before, either with your assistance or on their own. Your child can also set out the clothing they will need for school and any after-school activities.

- **Your child can use an alarm clock** now. They can also dress, groom, and feed themselves. Bear in mind, adolescents struggle to wake early. Studies show that their biorhythms change, so they are programmed to stay up later and sleep in longer. If your child's school does not take this into account by starting lessons later, suggest your child sets their alarm earlier to allow more time to wake up.

- **Encourage siblings of different ages** to work together. For example, an older sibling could get breakfast ready while the younger sibling feeds a pet. An older child could also help by brushing and tying back a younger one's hair.

- **Assign each person a task**—whether locking doors, turning off lights, or clearing food and dirty dishes—that needs to be taken care of before you can all leave the house.

- **Be prepared for journeys**. If you drive your child to school, who is driving? Who will buckle up young children? If your child takes public transportation, is their travel card ready?

Working together as a family to get ready in the mornings can be time-efficient and creates an atmosphere of mutual support.

MEALTIMES: YOUNG CHILDREN

From 18 months to 6 years of age, mealtimes evolve. In their first three years, you may choose to feed your child before you eat; however, the sooner you can eat some or all of your meals together, the greater the benefits for your child.

Early skills

Your young child will naturally eat smaller amounts of food and eat more often than you. As their feeding pattern starts to align with your own, and once they can feed themselves, provide a chair that they can safely sit in to join you at the family table. By their first birthday or before, they will probably be able to eat at the table with you, sharing family meals together.

By around 18 months old, your child becomes more skilled with their hands and fingers, alternating between eating with fingers and utensils, when food has been cut up. Teach them step by step how to use cutlery. Ideally, avoid plastic and use child-sized metal cutlery (see p.58). Start with a butter knife so they can learn to hold it correctly, apply soft spreads, and slice soft foods. By about 4 years of age, show them how to use a knife with a pointed edge to cut

through food that requires more control. Introducing utensils that are similar to the ones that you use makes your child feel empowered and helps them master real cutlery with safety and control.

Eating together

Encourage your young child to try new foods and eat a balanced diet. If they have strong preferences for unhealthy foods or resist a new food, recognize their preferences, limit how often you offer them, and continue to offer a range of healthy foods. Getting them involved in prepping meals can be helpful.

If your child refuses a meal you have made, acknowledge their opinion, then gently but consistently encourage them to try it. If they still refuse, they can join you at the table for mealtime conversation. Do not force them to eat, put a plate in front of them, prepare different food, or bribe them with dessert. Instead, let them know there is food if they change their mind and trust they will eat when hungry. If they become disruptive, invite them to visit their quiet place (see pp.156–159).

By 3 to 6 years of age, children are able to practice manners (see p.61) and put the Montessori principles of grace and courtesy into practice: eating carefully, engaging in mealtime conversations, and helping with cleaning up.

" "

As your child grows, they can learn that mealtimes provide a perfect opportunity to talk and engage together as a family.

Using child-sized metal cutlery encourages your child to practice the skills needed during mealtimes.

Cleaning faces and hands

Helping your young child clean themselves at the end of a meal can be a wonderful learning opportunity for them and a chance for you to provide gentle care. However, adults often tend to race through this part of the meal. They may quickly grab a face cloth, rush up behind their little one, hold onto their face from behind, and briskly wipe their child's face and hands. Imagine how unpleasant it would feel if someone bigger and stronger than you did the same thing to you. In addition, by doing this, your child does not learn anything about how to take care of themselves.

Instead, have on hand two warm, moist cloths—one for yourself and one for your child. Get down to their level, face to face. Show your child how you gently wipe your own face. Then let them try to wipe their face. If their face is not quite clean, finish off, wiping it gently and carefully for them, but only after they have had a try. Do the same to teach them how to clean their hands and fingers. You could have a bowl of clean, warm water on the table—out of your child's reach—to rinse the cloths between wiping your faces and hands. In this way, cleaning up after a meal will become a routine that your child looks forward to rather than dreads.

MEALTIMES: OLDER CHILDREN

As children grow, sitting down as a family and sharing food without screens or interruptions from phones is increasingly rare. Make a commitment to each other that mealtimes will be a period when you spend dedicated time together: work is set aside and calls or text messages are dealt with afterward.

A rewarding time

Eating with older children can be richly rewarding. These ideas and guidelines can help make mealtimes a treasured part of the day.

- **Dress up the table**. Favor sitting at a table instead of a breakfast bar. A touch of formality at times lends a festive spirit to meals.

- **Create a family circle**. If you wish, join hands and share a moment of silence, reflecting on the day. Say thank you for simple blessings, and thank the cook—not for how tasty the meal is, but to appreciate the effort that went into preparing it.

- **Check in with each other**. At the start of the meal, you might want to take turns, informally, to tell the rest of the family about your day. Family members can share anything they feel comfortable saying to the whole family. It might be something that went well, was a challenge, or was upsetting or stressful. There might be an area where someone feels they need to learn something new to be able to handle their work or social life more effectively. This can be a time to keep each other in the loop and, occasionally, to make a commitment to yourself or others in the family.

- **Have real conversations**. Current events, life, and work can be intriguing. Some families enjoy lively discussions at mealtimes. The key for parents is to listen and inquire, as much as to tell stories or teach lessons. If there is an awkward moment when no one has a topic of interest, allow this. After a short silence, your child may recall something they want to share.

- **Stick to topics everyone likes**. Notice what your family enjoys exploring. Your child may feel left out of conversations about adult matters that do not interest them, so make time to talk to your partner away from the table.

- **Help your child** continue to develop grace, courtesy, and manners (see p.61). Teach these from a positive perspective rather than scolding or shaming. Help them learn how to eat politely, sit up, pass items, and listen without interrupting. Teach awareness of others, for example, by not taking more than their share, and model how to ask to be excused gracefully if conversations go on for longer than they prefer.

- **If your child is in a play** or learning a poem, they might like to recite some lines. While Montessori avoids challenges that overwhelm a child's ability and makes them feel ashamed, it does recognize that memorizing lines is a useful skill. Many of us have snippets of poetry learned as children

that we treasure. Make the experience fun, not a burden. Gauge if your child loves it or would really rather avoid this.

- **In warmer months**, try to spend time outside after dinner to promote your child's appreciation of the natural world and extend this positive family time. Ideally, leave phones inside so you have everyone's attention. Notice the sun setting, collect leaves, play tag, feel an evening breeze, or just quietly talk.

Older children take an active role at meals, helping themselves to food and making sure others have what they need.

EVERYDAY STRATEGIES

NATURAL CONSEQUENCES

As parents, we are often reluctant to allow our children to experience the inevitable outcome of a wrong step or action. However, shielding children in this way means that they often fail to learn valuable life lessons.

A traditional approach to parenting has been to try to teach children lessons by lecturing and punishing them for perceived misbehavior and sometimes giving them no option but to behave in a certain way. However, the most common outcome of this approach is that children end up feeling as though they are disappointing their parents. When they are made to feel worse by punitive tactics, children do not tend to respond by reflecting on their behavior and improving it for the better.

Natural consequences are the best way to teach children, because consequences speak for themselves in many everyday situations. When parents do not interfere with natural consequences and allow children to experience the results of their actions, children tend to remember lessons better. In Montessori-inspired homes, parents use natural consequences often instead of assigning punishments or rescuing children from real-life lessons. Pages 84–85 outline helpful guidelines for using natural consequences.

" "

Children are more likely to learn lessons when they are allowed to experience the consequences of their actions.

" " OUR STORY

Jasmine, my 3-and-a-half-year-old, loves to make her own decisions. One chilly morning, we were getting dressed. We had nothing special planned—just spending time in the yard and around the house. When I asked her to put on extra layers so she didn't get cold outside, she danced off in the opposite direction, singing, "No, no, no, I don't like to wear those clothes! Oh no, no, no."

I knew she would be cold. However, rather than tell her that she would not be allowed outside without extra layers, I decided that using natural consequences on this occasion would be a far more helpful lesson. She pulled on her rain boots and headed outside without her coat. Within moments of playing in her mud "kitchen," she turned and asked, "Mom, where's the thing filled with hot water?" I looked at her and held back a smile. "Are you asking about the hot-water bottle?" I said. "Yes," she said, "I think I need it. My hands are cold and I'm shivering. I want to put my coat on."

My smile grew—I was so proud. The natural consequences technique had worked so well, and the best part was it had avoided causing conflict or hurting her feelings by insisting she wear her coat when she had made a choice not to. "Okay," I said to her, "let's go in; I'll get the hot-water bottle and you get your coat on." She looked up at me with her cold little hands outstretched, smiled, and said, "Thanks, Mom."

Chaneen (@chaneensaliee), mother of Jasmine, age 3, and Ocean, age 1

NATURAL CONSEQUENCES IN PRACTICE

Let the consequence speak

Take care to allow the consequence to teach the lesson instead of you—resist the temptation to point it out in advance. Telling your child ahead of time what the outcome of an action may be—for example, "If you forget your lunchbox, you'll be hungry"—ruins the effect of the experience.

Do not shame your child

After your child has experienced a natural consequence, do not rub this in or shame them, for example, by saying, "I told you that you would be hungry. If you had remembered your lunchbox, that would not have been the case." Your child is probably well aware of the result.

> ❝ ❞
>
> A natural consequence speaks for itself. There is no need to chastise or lecture.

Giving your child responsibility for certain tasks and actions can mean they learn by natural consequences.

Do not rescue your child

Avoid solving your child's problem, for example, by dropping off their lunch at school. Allowing the natural consequence often leads children to problem-solve and remember things instead of depending on you. A child whose parents always remember is likely to often forget.

Avoid punishments

Do not punish your child after a natural consequence. The consequence is enough to teach the lesson. For instance, if they do not get ready for bed in time, naturally this means there is not time for a story before lights out. Adding on a punishment—"There will be no more bedtime stories for a month!"—is most likely to make your child feel resentful and act out.

When to avoid this strategy

The following are clear occasions when natural consequences should not be used.

If your child could be harmed. For example, you would not let a young child near a hot stove to feel the heat in order to teach them not to touch it.

The consequence is too removed from the action. For instance, if your child is in charge of watering a houseplant and forgets to do so, do not expect them to connect it dying two weeks later with this action.

If an action harms property or others. For example, your child learns not to kick a ball inside if it damages walls or hurts someone, but this lesson comes at a cost to your home and others.

If your child does not care about the result. For example, you may decide to let them feel a little hungry for a while if they do not come to dinner when asked, but this will not work if they had a big snack before dinner.

LEAVING FOR THE DAY

Leaving for the day, whether to go to a caregiver, daycare, or school, is a time of transition in your child's daily routine. Being organized, punctual, and positive helps your child start their day confidently.

The importance of punctuality

Getting ready each day (see pp.74–77), leaving the house on time when traveling to daycare or school, and undertaking a journey all teach your child valuable life lessons. They are learning to separate from you to keep themselves safe, grow in independence, and develop a sense of responsibility.

Being punctual is a key life lesson. Your child learns this by arriving at school on time—having navigated their morning routine with your help—and by learning that they can count on you to pick them up punctually each day. Being on time for arrival and pick-up and ensuring that your child knows who is meeting them helps them feel emotionally secure and confident.

The journey

Taking your young child to daycare or school can provide wonderful moments—you may engage in a conversation, your child may spend time reading if you are driving, or you might observe the sunrise or enjoy seeing plants and animals in the natural world on your walk.

You may also need to manage stressful moments. Giving children allocated roles can help avoid flash points. For example, if your child resists wearing a seatbelt, putting them in charge of ensuring that everyone is buckled up, including themselves, gives them a sense of responsibility and helps them understand the importance of this task.

If siblings squabble on the way, simply stop, if possible, then make it clear to them that you will resume the journey when they are ready to converse quietly and respectfully.

Ages and stages

18 months–6 years
Help very young children with tasks such as putting on shoes, dressing, and gathering their lunch and belongings. Your goal is for them to become increasingly independent during these years and to care for themselves.

6–12 years
Now that your child can manage practical skills, put more emphasis on them taking responsibility for organizing themselves.

12–18 years
As teens focus on friends, activities, and social lives, their minds can become somewhat chaotic and disorganized, and there may be a lack of attention to detail. Offer renewed support, if needed, to help keep them on track.

A positive start to the day

Some young children may experience a degree of separation anxiety when they are dropped off at daycare or school. This is a normal part of early development. As they get older, they may become anxious again when starting a new school or activity, if they are concerned about exams, or if there is conflict with a peer. Some supportive strategies can help:

- **Visit your child's** new caregiver, daycare, or school with them before they start so they can see their new environment and meet staff or carers and other children. If possible, arrange a play date with another family so your child knows someone from the outset.

- **Be honest with a young child** to build trust. When you leave, be positive about their day, let them know where you are going and when you will be back, then say a quick goodbye.

- **As they grow**, agree where and when to say "goodbye"—at the school entrance, on the way, or at home. Send them off on a positive note, encouraging their skills and talents.

- **Your child may be apprehensive** when starting secondary school. Encourage them to share any concerns. Listen without offering solutions or sympathy. Talking things through can help them find their own solution. If they ask for advice, offer suggestions in question form; for example, "I wonder what would happen if you told your new friend how you feel?" Your child needs a listening ear, advice if requested, and guidance on safety and ethics. Beyond this, making their own mistakes helps them learn.

Getting packed and ready the night before promotes good timekeeping skills.

FREE TIME AND WEEKENDS: YOUNG CHILDREN

At 18 months, the structure of each day should be similar for your child to provide consistency and routine. Keep mealtimes, naps, and bedtimes on weekends as close to their weekday schedule as possible. As they grow, children become able to cope with more flexible routines on weekends.

Family time

When your child is young, family life on weekends and school vacations is likely to be simple and not overly structured. However, leisure time does allow you to spend time together on family activities both at and away from home and to introduce new experiences and people into your child's life. In these formative

Tackling tasks together helps build strong family connections.

years, your child will get to know extended family members and friends, forming lasting bonds, for example, with grandparents.

Natural activities for children

In the early years, the leisure time activities you plan with your child can support their physical, social, and emotional development and help them learn important life skills. Choose activities that promote hand–eye coordination and brain development and ones that involve working in collaboration to develop social skills and build strong family connections.

- **Your young child** is building strength and coordination. Engage them in activities that develop large muscle control, balance, coordination, and muscle tone and that teach them to enjoy moving. Try moving quickly or slowly to music together, singing, or doing yoga. They could walk heel-to-toe while carrying an object—often practiced in Montessori schools. Play games where you mirror their actions as they move their legs or hands, or vice versa. Or set up an indoor or outdoor obstacle course.

- **Set aside time** for your child to join you on projects. Hobbies such as woodwork

Quiet time

Young children are naturally active. It is important to balance their time with quiet activities during free time, just as you would on weekdays, such as listening to music together or sharing a story.

Build in time, too, for your child to occupy themselves. They can play quietly near you while you are busy with tasks. As well as giving you time to get jobs done or follow your own interests, this also helps your child learn to make choices for themselves.

develop hand–eye coordination. Around the age of 4, children can start to use child-sized tools, such as a small hammer or child-safe saw, wearing safety goggles and supervised by you.

- **Use extra time on weekends** to spend time in the kitchen with your child. Cooking or baking projects— such as making soup from scratch or baking bread, pizza, or cookies—are ideal for parents and young children. Take your time to teach them basic prepping and cooking skills.

- **Plan family activities**, whether clearing leaves, enjoying a walk, or working on an art project together.

FREE TIME AND WEEKENDS: OLDER CHILDREN

As your child grows beyond the early childhood years, your family's free time, weekends, and vacations might change as your child's interests, needs, and level of independence evolve. Ensuring you continue to spend time with them while also allowing them to expand their interests is a question of balance.

After-school activities are a great outlet and help children learn about sensible scheduling.

The need for balance

As your child grows, after-school and weekend activities and, increasingly, a desire to spend more time with friends, often away from home, compete for their time. Avoid overscheduling free time now, because this can create overload for all. Build in time with your child by watching or taking part in some of their activities and enjoying outings together. Bear in mind that each family member needs time to relax, do chores, and follow their own interests.

A family discussion

To promote balance and understanding, use family meetings to discuss whether new activities can comfortably fit in with existing plans. Discuss how they impact each person. Make decisions that take into account what is important to you all: what do we have time for, how much will it cost, and is it within our budget? This helps your child think about others, decide what they really value, and understand how much goes into making decisions about their activities.

- **Involve your child fully** in choosing their extracurricular activities. Discuss the cost, travel time, whether a new activity will interfere with family commitments, and the overall time

66 99 OUR STORY

Having four children and being part of a community within the school, church, and neighborhood, all involving extracurricular activities, we saw that our lives were going to get busier than we knew would be healthy for us.

My wife and I made the choice to carve out family time each week. Saturday become a family fun day, dedicated to time just for us to spend the day together, primarily at home, with bike rides, walks, reading books, enjoying games, cooking, baking, and eating. Occasionally, we will have outings to a zoo, restaurant, or another place that we view as a treat. Sunday, after church, we treat as a rest day and also do necessary household chores, with exceptions made for out-of-town visitors or special celebrations and gatherings.

David, father of Eden age 10, Eli age 8, Ewan age 6, and Ethan age 4

commitment that would be required from each family member.

- **Even activities or classes** that you feel are non-negotiable, such as those related to education, faith, or culture, are best discussed openly so your child understands why they are important.

- **Consider limits**. These may focus on whether you feel an activity is safe. You can also set limits to help children learn about commitments rather than bounce arbitrarily between activities. For example, if they want music lessons, agree on a time commitment so you do not sign up for a series of lessons, only for them to want to drop out several weeks later.

In adolescence especially, these discussions are key. Adolescents want to separate from parents, feeling they are individuals with their own voice. Talking and debating ideas keeps communication open and promotes understanding. Adolescents need to be able to make choices, but parents need to help them see the ramifications. If they insist, at times you may have to allow them to experience the consequences of choosing unwisely.

MANAGING SCREEN TIME: YOUNG CHILDREN

From the very start of your child's life, talk to your parenting partner about how much screen time your child will be allowed. Review your own screen time habits now, too, bearing in mind that your habits and behavior set an example for your child. Work out some screen house rules for the whole family (see p.96).

Your child's influences

Children's values and knowledge about the world have traditionally been shaped by five cultural influences: home, school, youth groups and activities, faith-based organizations, and peers. Television has also competed for children's attention, joined today by games and apps on digital devices and consoles, social media, and online videos, which represent a sixth, incredibly powerful culture over which many parents have limited knowledge and exercise little control. Face-to-face communication is increasingly sacrificed as even young children are silent and absorbed in their digital devices.

Types of learning

Slick marketing often sets out to convince parents that babies and young children learn faster when exposed to technology. However, studies suggest that they learn best by interacting with hands-on, three-dimensional materials;

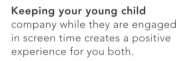

Keeping your young child company while they are engaged in screen time creates a positive experience for you both.

from real-world experiences; and from other people. When writing about children under 6 years old, Montessori said, "Never give something to the mind before you give it to the hand." Today, brain research confirms this fundamental principle. For young children, the physical act of counting out forks and knives, pouring juice, or building a puzzle provides a more solid learning base than interacting with a two-dimensional screen with a finger or a mouse.

A balanced approach

If you think some digital media, apps, and television programs could have some value for your child, aim to keep the time they spend in front of a screen to a minimum and use this time as an opportunity to interact with them. You might snuggle up and read an e-book or watch a children's program together.

Avoid relying on digital devices to keep your child calm and quiet or as a way to occupy them while you are busy. This could lead to them becoming dependent on technology rather than human beings for comfort and care.

Be aware, too, that screen time can have long-term consequences for your young child's ability to attend to tasks. Studies show that children who engage with digital devices and televisions daily

from 1 to 3 years old are more likely to find it hard to focus once at school. Children and adults can experience symptoms of addiction from excessive screen time, and screen time and digital devices can also interfere with sleep. Moderation and balance when using screens is key to supporting happy, healthy relationships, learning, and positive behavior.

Screen time recommendations

The following guidelines can help you regulate your young child's screen time:

- From birth to 2 years, keep screen time to a minimum. If possible, no screen time is best. For 3- to 6-year-olds, limit screen time to one to two hours a day. Other screens nearby should be counted in your child's screen time, as younger children constantly absorb the stimuli around them.

- Be very selective before introducing technology into your child's life. Watch and listen to programs and games and gauge their appropriateness.

- Spend screen-free time with your child.

- Treat technology as a tool, not a toy, especially below the age of 6.

- Make agreements with others close to your child about the use of technology around and with your child.

MANAGING SCREEN TIME: OLDER CHILDREN

From elementary school years up through adolescence, technology and digital media can be useful when your child is researching a subject, and games and videos can be a valued source of entertainment. However, problems can arise if there is unlimited access to screens without attention to the quality of the material.

A healthy balance

As your child grows, they may need to use a computer or tablet to help with work. However, you may want to agree to a time limit on the amount of free time they spend on screens. Use family meetings to discuss a balance between sedentary activities and physical and interactive ones. Drawing up house rules (see p.96) can be helpful.

The hazards of screen time

It is easy for children and adults to lose a sense of time and reality when looking at a screen—whether passively consuming content, which requires little effort, or engaged in social media or games, which can become addictive. Be aware that you are modeling behavior and try to avoid being absorbed in your own devices when together as a family.

You will need to make decisions constantly about what to allow into your home, so think carefully about the level of violence your child is exposed to, from enacted murders to fights, crashes, and explosions. The values and problem-solving approaches in media aimed at children are often very different from those of a Montessori-inspired home.

Quality screen time

Some basic guidelines can help you select programming that enhances your child's understanding of the world; ignites awareness, curiosity, and imagination in a positive manner; and hopefully reinforces your positive values.

- **Documentaries**—whether about nature, science, history, space, or technology—can be educational, informative, and at times age specific. Avoid "educational" children's programs that promote learning by memorization rather than fostering understanding of concepts or ideas.

- **Choose movies and shows** that present compelling stories and characters, whether fictional, biographical, or portraying a time or event in history. Montessori aims to limit exposure to unrealistic, fantastical stories, even though some can be positive and entertaining. Expose your child to stories that showcase respect and kindness and have a positive but realistic message.

- **Avoid content** that is misleading; filled with sarcasm and ridicule; humor based on a character being embarrassed or hurt; or undermines family values that aim to teach children to be advocates for justice, kindness, compassion, and peaceful conflict resolution.

- **Think about content**. Research games, movies, and shows on trusted online guides for families to make sure

they are age-appropriate. Look for quality content, too, just as you would with reading material. Choose videos that are enjoyable, clear, appear to be accurate, do not glorify cruelty or violence, and do not contain sexual situations that would make you or your child feel awkward.

- **Use family meetings** to help your child understand why your family's values on digital content may be in conflict with their friend's family values.

Exposing your child to programs that adhere to your core family values is a great way to promote positive messages.

HOUSE RULES FOR SCREEN TIME

Prioritize reaching a general consensus about the use of digital devices and media for different age levels as soon as possible. Aim to strike a balance between access to digital media and enjoying a family life that supports your values.

The role of house rules

It is important to create house rules around digital devices and the media that you are comfortable allowing your child to engage with. When they are young, it is easy to draw up rules. As children grow, they will question and debate why rules are needed, so establishing house rules that make sense and that you are willing to follow is key. While the rules will no doubt need adapting as your child grows, they should be based on your family values, be fair, and be followed consistently. They should recognize that time spent on screens can be positive but should not interfere with family connections or tasks. Be sure that others who spend time with your child, such as grandparents, friends, or babysitters, know the rules.

Family time without digital distractions shows children how to balance activities.

Be a good role model and follow your family's house rules for digital devices and media. Consider the following:

- **Put your smartphone** away when dropping off and picking up your child, and avoid nonessential phone calls when traveling with them.

- **As with any life situation** that could harm your child, prepare them to keep themselves safe by discussing internet safety rules.

- **Avoid screens in bedrooms**. They can interfere with sleep, expose children to unwanted content, and pull them away from interacting with others.

- **Learn how to use** parental control software to limit your child's screen time and access to concerning content.

- **Set up media-free** family time, when you focus on reading; games; or real-life experiences such as mealtimes, bedtime, and outings.

- **Ensure children spend** as much time each day reading, exercising, and playing as they do on a screen.

- **If a rule is broken**, discuss consequences that are reasonable, respectful, responsible, and related.

- **Know what your child** is watching and listening to and talk about it with them.

Using social media safely

Be guided by your family values when talking to your child about using social media safely and thoughtfully, and think about how you use it, too.

- Discuss being thoughtful before posting online photos or videos. Could they embarrass them one day or compromise the family's privacy? Apply this principle to yourself before posting images of your child.

- Exercise caution when texting. Texting takes away two important aspects of communication: you cannot see the recipient or hear their tone of voice. This makes it hard to interpret messages that involve emotions, leading to misunderstandings. Suggest your child sticks to messages that give information and saves those that involve emotions for face-to-face conversations.

- Discuss hazards such as the addictive nature of social media; making or receiving mean-spirited comments, which can step over into online bullying; presenting a more exciting life than is the reality; and the risk of connecting with a stranger who may present a danger.

- Avoid "overparenting." While helpful, technology can mean parents communicate with and monitor their children too much. This can inhibit children from practicing life skills such as problem solving and remembering, which increase confidence in their ability to care for themselves when away from you and help them develop a strong sense of autonomy.

BEDTIME: YOUNG CHILDREN

Sleeping arrangements for babies and toddlers are a topic of debate and are influenced by a family's beliefs, culture, and values. In a Montessori-inspired home, parents strive to help children become independent, including when going to sleep. There are no strict rules, but the aim is for them to settle themselves and sleep on their own. By the age of 6, their bedtime routine will be well established.

Independent sleeping

Your child's sleep environment helps them learn to sleep independently.

- Once your toddler begins to try to climb out of their crib, lower the sides so that they can get in and out safely. When you feel they are ready, move them to a child's bed or a regular-size single bed.

- From about 18 months until 3 years old, a gate in the bedroom door helps your child stay in their room at night. Ensure that the room is completely safe in case they wake up and are alone. This safe environment encourages independence.

- Some young children might want a prop to help them sleep independently. A nightlight and/or a soft toy can be reassuring and comforting.

- Most children settle down more easily in a calm, uncluttered bedroom (see pp.56–57), following a nightly routine.

Winding down

Moving from active play to a quiet and calm state, ready for sleep, can be a difficult transition for your child.

Young children can be overstimulated by a lot of activity around them, time spent looking at or being near screens, or loud noise in the house at bedtime.

After your child's evening meal, choose soothing activities. A warm bath, a story, or just snuggling in a comfy chair can all help your child feel ready for sleep. Be cautious about props or actions for soothing infants and toddlers, such as using a motorized swing or rocking an infant or toddler in your arms until they are asleep. While these can be calming, you should put your child in their bed before they fall asleep so that they become used to being put down awake and falling asleep alone.

By about 3 years of age, your child can be more actively involved in their bedtime routine. To help them transition from playtime to bedtime, you could encourage a habit of getting ready for bed earlier. This can become a looked-forward-to time where they engage in quiet activities such as looking at books—with you or on their own—before getting into bed or cuddling a favorite soft toy. By 5 or 6 years of age, children can usually read quietly by themselves in bed with the lights on.

" "

Bedtime is a time of transition
for your young child that
requires a change of pace
to help them settle down.

Developing habits such as
quietly reading at bedtime
gives children helpful tools
for settling down to sleep.

Settling down to sleep

How you say goodnight to your child
and handle nighttime waking plays an
important part in encouraging them to
settle down and sleep independently.

- **A comforting routine** can be tucking
  them in, saying goodnight, then
  returning for "whispers" and lights off
  as they settle. Whispering messages
  of love creates an intimacy that sends
  them to sleep feeling cherished.

- **At 18 months to 2 years**, if your child
  wakes, go to their room quietly, but do
  not pick them up or move them to your
  room. Wait a minute or two to see if
  they settle. If you feel they need help,
  spend a few minutes gently talking to
  them. Say it is still night and sleep time.
  From about 3 years, if your child
  wakes from a bad dream, reassure them
  calmly that you understand it was scary,
  but you are there and their room is safe.

BEDTIME: OLDER CHILDREN

In elementary, middle, and high school years, bedtime routines evolve. Help children associate the bedroom with a place to relax and sleep. Ensure that their environment promotes good habits and ideally avoids screen time interfering with their sleep, health, and development.

Adapting bedtime

During the elementary school years, children may push for a later bedtime. As they approach adolescence, they often stay up increasingly late in defiance of wishes. Research suggests that there is a neurological basis for a teenager's tendency to stay up later. Teenagers may also enjoy staying up late, because this is something they were not allowed to do when younger.

Your goal is to ensure that throughout elementary school and adolescence, children continue to get adequate rest. Discuss a nighttime routine that helps your child prepare for sleep at a reasonable time, adapting this as they get older. Adolescents in particular are eager not to miss out on online activities and social media chats with peers. Talk to them about how to navigate this, explaining that friends will still be happy to chat the following day, and help them find ways to sign off at night with friends. Helping them let go and make good choices is a valuable lesson.

A healthy bedtime routine

It is important that children maintain good nighttime routines. Adopting a firm policy that digital devices are kept out of bedrooms when winding down is advised. It is wise to set a rule when your child is very young to not allow devices in the bedroom, because once they are allowed, it is hard to establish in your child's mind that at bedtime the bedroom is a place to sleep and dress. It can also

How technology affects sleep

Consider the following when thinking about the effect of technology on your child's sleep.

- Be mindful of how flashing lights and noise affect our brains as we drift off to sleep. Falling asleep to bright images from a digital device or the sound of a television can affect our ability to reach the calm, deep sleep we need to restore ourselves.

- Social media and online games can be addictive, and watching movies and surfing the net can lead a child to stay awake late into the night.

- Gaming devices let children play in real time with players in different time zones who are also complete strangers.

be difficult to monitor what they watch or do online when this takes place behind a closed door. Digital devices are also very stimulating and tend to keep our brains active, making it difficult to fall asleep.

If you find consistently enforcing this policy proves difficult, at least strive to have a clear lights-out policy that you check up on. You could say that all digital technology should be turned off and left outside of the bedroom after a certain time, adjusting this time as children get older.

Recommendations from sleep experts on how to prepare for sleep include:

- **Dim the bedroom lights**.
- **Advise your child** to use their bed only for calming activities that help with falling asleep.
- **For older children**, recommend that they turn music off or down before bedtime.
- **If older children** consume caffeine, they should avoid this after 2 p.m.
- **If adolescents wake during the night**, advise them to get out of bed without waking others and quietly do something relaxing.

❝ ❞

Bedtime routines will naturally evolve as children grow but should still be designed to promote adequate and restful sleep.

Keeping phones in a designated place at night, away from bedrooms, can be a family rule.

HELPING AT HOME

Family life is where children learn the basic skills of living with others and taking care of a home environment. Those habits and skills form a foundation for the rest of their lives.

Montessori teaching believes that children learn what they live—that is, they learn from their daily experiences. The everyday tasks involved in family living help children learn how to understand, appreciate, and work together with other members of the family—to be an active member of the family community. We all have our own distinct personalities and ways of approaching everyday life. By finding ways to work together, your child learns how to be part of a team, a skill that will help them throughout life—in study, during work, and when establishing a family of their own.

" "

Caring for the home environment is part of what defines being in a family community, with each family member taking responsibility for tasks.

SKILLS FOR LIFE

We want children to understand that, while we love them, we expect them to help out. This teaches them about structure, shared responsibility, how we depend on one another, the value of teamwork, and the importance of doing a job well.

Working together

Your young child's concept of how to do a task will not, necessarily, match yours. Initially, you are teaching them how to do a job step by step. If they make a mistake, repeat a lesson without shame or blame, but with firm, gentle encouragement. As they grow, keep the following in mind:

With your help and guidance, very young children often embrace the chance to help around the home, working close to you.

- **Your child's sense of time** is not the same as yours. Children under the age of 6 often become distracted, showing the natural tendency of young children to live in the moment.

- **Young children** may be more focused on the process rather than completing a job. Recognize their contribution and progress, appreciating that it takes time for them to develop lifelong habits.

- **Your child needs** to be independent and feel valued, both great motivators. Instead of thinking of chores as onerous tasks, see them as an opportunity for your child to contribute meaningfully.

- **Young children** especially enjoy being with us. They participate not just to make you happy, but to be at your side. Harness this desire to get them into a pattern of routine tasks, working in harmony as you teach them skills.

- **As your child grows**, they may have more schoolwork and activities. It is completely reasonable to expect them to continue contributing to chores and to build these into their schedule.

COOKING

A large part of the enjoyment of any meal is involvement in the preparation of the food. Montessori emphasizes how important it is to allow children to have a meaningful part in family life as soon as they are able to.

Scaffolding skills

When guided by patient adults and given the right tools, even very young children can help prepare food. For instance, your toddler can learn to peel a tangerine or use a butter knife to slice a banana or spread peanut butter. As your child becomes increasingly dexterous with their hands and fingers, they can master more complex cooking skills and also combine skills. So your 5-year-old can use newly acquired reading skills to follow simple recipes, and as your child grows, they can use their increased understanding and abilities to follow multistep recipes, to double or triple ingredients, and to become more independent in the kitchen.

Working alongside each other independently—ready to guide if needed—builds your child's confidence in their skills and ability.

" "
Cooking with children can be messy. Take it slowly and think of spills as part of the process, teaching them to mop, wipe, and sweep.

Planning ahead

Preparation and thought enhance the joy of cooking with your child, allowing you both to concentrate on the process and working together rather than being frustrated if ingredients are not available or you need to hunt for a tool midstep. Your child can also learn self-preparation— how to wash their hands, put on an apron, and cover their hair or tie it back.

- **Provide proper tools**—blunt knives can be more dangerous than sharp ones—and show how equipment is used to slice, grate, or peel safely.

- **Let your child know** that they must have your permission or supervision when using the oven or stove.

- **Prep ingredients**. Help your child understand the importance of following recipes and measuring, especially for baking. But flag up chances for creativity, too, such as when making a fruit salad.

A complete task

Montessori teaches that tasks have a beginning, middle, and end, so cleaning is an important part of cooking. Cleaning up together as you go along teaches your child to do this methodically. This then ceases to be overwhelming, instilling the skill in a manageable way and ensuring that your child cleans up automatically each time.

Using a butter knife helps your child safely learn skills such as chopping at a young age.

Ages and stages

18 months–6 years
Hands are the first tools. Start with foods that your child can prep by hand, such as peeling an orange. As they grow, they can use a butter knife to slice soft foods such as bananas, celery, or cucumber and to apply spreads. From as early as 3 years, they can peel with a peeler or apple cutter, progressing to a sharp knife. Your child can also make a fruit salad; prepare biscuits, flatbreads, or muffins following a simple recipe; and add skills by baking with yeast.

6–12 years
Your child may be quite skilled now and creative. They can prepare a variety of foods using more complex tools, such as a food processor, electric mixer; and, with supervision, the oven. They can also read and follow recipes with multiple steps and double, triple, or halve a recipe using math skills.

12–18 years
Give scope for your child to fill a leadership role—budgeting for a meal, expanding a recipe, and inviting guests. Encourage them to make a range of food, from omelets to fish, roasted vegetables, soups, and desserts.

CLEANING AND FAMILY CHORES

As with daily routines and other family structures, children can begin to help out with everyday chores at a much earlier age than most parents ever imagine. Encouraging your child to get involved with household jobs facilitates their independence.

How your child can help

Children can begin to help out with chores as young as 2 or 3 years old. If tasks are introduced correctly, your child not only learns useful skills, but also understands that everyone pitches in. A child-sized broom or mop are useful tools for your young child. However, there are many ways they can help out without needing special equipment. For example, they can make their bed, put dirty clothes in the laundry, fold clean clothes, wipe and dust, water indoor plants, and help in the kitchen. As they grow, they can also learn to use equipment such as the vacuum cleaner or the kitchen mop to keep the house clean.

Getting your child involved

Think about your child and their abilities and consider what they are ready to help with and what they show interest in. Rather than tell a very young child that it is their job to do something, instead, deliberately organize your home so they

Everyday tasks, such as washing and drying dishes, provide an opportunity for children to work together and learn basic skills.

Feeling in charge of a task can be a good motivator for a child and builds their confidence.

Ages and stages

18 months–6 years

Most young children want to do what you do and can enjoy tasks that we see as chores. If wiping the table, they are likely to be more interested in wetting a cloth, wiping, rinsing the cloth, and drying the table than in ensuring the table is clean. Let them enjoy the process.

6–12 years

Teach your child more advanced skills now, such as removing stains, vacuuming, scrubbing pans, and cleaning the car to help them feel a sense of ownership and pride in their home.

12–18 years

Teens may prefer to be with friends, study, or focus on other activities. Use family meetings to keep them focused on the need to share in household chores as they prepare for adulthood.

can safely and easily work with you. For example, if they enjoy taking things out and putting them back, work together to unload clothes from the dryer into the laundry basket.

As your child grows, they may express a desire to be involved. At around 4 or 5 years old, you may notice that they are developing routines around small jobs. As well as engineering your home so they know where tools for helping out are and can access them, talk to them about how much you value their contribution. Agree on some initial jobs to do routinely together, or that they might do on their own. Once they master a task, give simple reminders. For example, if they learn how to water a houseplant, encourage them to check it daily to see if it is dry, explaining that overwatering drowns the roots.

Suggest this could become one of their jobs. Agree to a list of regular tasks for each family member at a family meeting.

If your older child is a reluctant helper, this may be a sign that they struggle with a task or are avoiding it. Try giving them ownership of a task. For example, if they fail to put dirty clothes in the laundry, put them in charge of making sure that everyone does this. This gives them a feeling of leadership and responsibility.

EVERYDAY STRATEGIES
DISARMING SQUABBLES

Disagreements are part of life, and dealing with conflict is a learning process. As parents, our role is to guide children through conflict with a sibling, cousin, or friend to help them reach a peaceful resolution.

Peaceful conflict resolution skills are valuable throughout life. The sooner children learn these skills, the more independent they can be in working out disagreements by themselves. They also become better at listening to others' needs and expressing their own. Your role is to help your child learn to solve problems peacefully and independently rather than to judge and come up with solutions. At times, you may be able to prevent conflict from escalating by simply doing something comical or unexpected to break the tension. Or children may be able to solve a situation without your help. Resist the urge to jump in. Instead, give them a minute to see if a disagreement calms down or escalates. If it escalates, try the strategies on pages 110–111; these deal with conflict both in the moment and, when emotions are too high to problem-solve on the spot, show you how to take a break and follow through later to ensure that ongoing conflict is resolved.

Holding hands is one of the simplest ways to help children listen to each other and resolve disagreements.

" " **OUR STORY**

When my children were 6 and 10 years old, they had a brain teaser puzzle and were both fascinated by it. Quickly, this puzzle game became the center of attention and they fought over it frequently.

To find a fair solution about how to share this favorite toy, I waited for a moment when they were both calm, then sat them down, and we brainstormed some solutions for how they might take turns with the puzzle.

It was decided that the toy would stay downstairs on a shelf so that it was available for both of them to play with. They agreed that once one of them was having a turn playing with it, they could continue playing with it for as long as they wanted to during that play session. When they had finished, they had to return it to its place on the shelf so that it was available for their sibling.

My daughter wrote down the rule on a piece of paper, which they both signed. They shook hands to show their agreement, and the "contract" was hung on the shelf next to the toy. I was impressed by how well they responded to the conflict resolution strategy.

Carine (@montessorifamilyuk), mother of Louis, age 9 and Lily, age 13

DISARMING SQUABBLES IN PRACTICE

1
Be a calming presence

Move close to the two squabbling parties, doing this slowly and calmly. Once you are close, get down to the children's eye level and look at them both calmly and kindly so they understand that you are not going to become part of the conflict.

2
Be gently authoritative

Put a hand gently on each of them to help calm them, then just wait for them to stop squabbling. If they are arguing over an object, when they begin to calm down, hold out your hand to signal that you want the item in question. Do not speak until they give it to you.

3
Express your thanks

Thank them for ending the squabble. If children were arguing over an object or a toy that they have handed to you, put this to one side. This signals that you have not confiscated it, but they should return to it only when they can do so peacefully.

4
Show belief

Assure both parties that you are confident they can work out whatever it was they were squabbling about and find a solution together that they are both happy with. Allow them the time and space they need for this problem-solving process.

" "

Gently guiding children on conflict resolution gives them the skills to resolve disputes independently in the future.

5
Take a break if needed

If either child is simply too upset to engage in solving the dispute on the spot, ask both parties to take a break, then follow through later to find a solution. When ready, ask them to hold hands—this action has a calming effect on the whole body.

6
Help them listen and talk

While they are holding hands, guide each child to take turns listening and talking to each other, reassuring them that they will each have a chance to talk. Take care not to judge the situation yourself or to offer ready-made solutions.

7
Get them to say how they feel

Help children through the process step by step so they learn to speak for themselves and express their feelings and ideas. For example, ask the first child to tell you why they are upset and how they feel. Acknowledge their feelings. Then ask them to tell the other child how they felt and what they would like them to do, such as return a pen.

8
Help them find a resolution

Ask the second child to give their side; maybe they needed the pen and it was not being used. Ask them to think about how they could resolve the dispute. For example, could they ask for the pen politely? Invite them to try this. If this does not work, continue to guide the children, suggesting they take a break if needed and return to the dispute later. Follow this through.

GARDENING

Nurturing a garden, or finding an opportunity for your child to enjoy gardening in a community, can be an invaluable experience for them. As well as showing them how to save money by growing high-quality fresh produce, they will also be surrounded by beauty and will learn about the seasons, ecosystems, and nature.

Ages and stages

18 months–6 years
Your child learns basic tasks in a very experiential way now. With child-sized tools and gloves, they can use a trowel and help you dig and hoe. They can plant seeds, rake, weed, and gather ripe produce.

6–12 years
The garden is a living laboratory for the natural world now. From water systems for maintaining growth, to seasonal changes, to the systems and cycles of living things, the science of nature stimulates your child's mind and raises their awareness of the impact of humans on nature.

12–18 years
Adolescents should continue to help out in the garden. They may become interested in different types of gardening, such as organic versus the use of pesticides and fertilizers. Encourage them to explore their values and beliefs.

Creative spaces
Gardening can be enjoyed in a variety of spaces. If you have a garden, you can set aside a small plot for your child to grow produce. Alternatively, grow edible and decorative plants indoors in containers, on a balcony, by windows or in window boxes, and even under grow lights. Or find out about sharing a space in a community garden or signing up for an allotment.

Nurturing your space
Gardens are a natural classroom. Whatever space you have available, encouraging your child to help out in the garden provides them with numerous learning opportunities. Getting involved in gardening also helps children form a deep sense of connection to—and appreciation for—the natural world.

- **Children can learn** practical skills, such as how to start seeds off indoors and then transplant the seedlings outside to grow at the correct time of the year.

- **Teach your child** how to take care of the garden and plants. At a family meeting, discuss how to share the responsibility of caring for all the living things in the garden. Depending on your child's age, they can help out with tasks such as watering, weeding, and harvesting with help or independently.

Working together with older siblings or parents helps children learn how to nurture and care for plants.

- **Planning a garden** or garden plot helps your child learn math skills and graphing. Work with them to measure the area available for growing plants. Draw a map and calculate the space needed for each plant when mature and the number of plants that will fit in the space.

- **As your child observes nature**, they can expand and enrich their vocabulary by learning the names of the parts of flowers and plants and by identifying flowers, plants, seeds, vegetables, herbs, and insects. You can also teach them the names of local wildflowers and trees.

- **Your child can explore processes**, life cycles, and insect communities. Indoors or outside, you can set up a small composting bin or a worm or ant farm. If you find a cocoon or chrysalis on a small branch, your child can observe it from day to day in place or take it indoors and set it in a suitable container to wait for the moth or butterfly to emerge.

- **The garden is a science lab**. Your child can witness and appreciate the web of life; the seasons; the weather; and, of course, botany. They can learn the difference between the plants you deliberately grow and weeds.

113

PETS

Our pets offer us companionship, love, and loyalty and give our children the chance to learn how to care for them. If you have a family pet or are thinking of getting one, you will need to model how to care for it, guiding your child on how to treat a pet, the responsibilities involved in caring for it, and how to cope with the experience of illness and possibly death.

Choosing a pet

It is important to be very thoughtful when considering getting a family pet. First, bear in mind the age of your child. If you have a pet when your child is born, they will grow up learning how to interact with and care for it. If you do not already have a pet, it is advisable to wait until your child is at least 4 years old. By this age, most children have enough maturity and self-control to be able to welcome a new animal safely. Discuss choosing a pet at a family meeting or over several family meetings. Think together about the space,

" "

Choosing a pet should be a carefully considered decision, discussed and agreed on by each family member.

Learning how to handle and care for a family pet teaches your child important lessons about responsibility and kindness.

time, and attention you can give a pet and research different animals. Help your child learn about the nature and care of dogs, cats, and smaller caged pets. Talking to them about a pet's needs and what is realistic for your family in terms of the space you can offer a pet helps them understand the care involved, the role they will be expected to play, and why it is important to think about the pet's needs first and whether you can meet them. Before you make a decision, consider your child's instincts and personality. Some animals are better around children than others, and vice versa.

Caring for pets

Your child will naturally learn how to care for your pet by watching you do this. Involve your child in a pet's care by allowing them to feed or water them, clean their cage, or brush them.

Spending time with a pet—whether playing with them, walking them, teaching them tricks, caring for them, or helping socialize a new pet into your home— provides invaluable lessons for your child. When caring for an animal, your child learns about kindness and empathy and about being careful in their movements so a pet is not hurt, dropped, or played with roughly. They also learn about compassion and the responsibility of caring for a dependent creature and about respect for all creatures.

Ages and stages

18 months–6 years
Young children can begin to help parents and older siblings care for family pets, for example, by setting out a bowl of water or accompanying another family member when walking the dog. They can learn to play with a pet with care and consideration.

6–12 years
As children grow, they gradually learn more about the responsibility of caring for pets. They can help with grooming and training. You can encourage your child's interest in the biology and care of your pet's species.

12–18 years
Be clear you expect your teen to carry on helping care for family pets. Some teens may want to learn more about animals and animal care and may express interest, for example, in volunteering at an animal shelter or getting involved in training and competitions. Encourage their interests.

Losing a pet

If a pet dies, your family will join together in the grieving process. This may be your child's first experience with such a difficult life situation. It is important to talk to them about how they are feeling. You can discuss your family's beliefs and guide them on moving forward while still remembering and honoring the pet they have lost.

LEARNING AT HOME

Your child is learning from birth, if not before, and will continue to learn throughout their life. We learn through our experiences— the things your child encounters daily will shape their learning.

You are and always will be your child's most important teacher. Some families choose to homeschool their children. Whether or not you do this, your child will still learn informally from you during the time you spend together. How you act and speak—both consciously and unconsciously—will inevitably influence your child. They will hear what you say; observe what you do; and participate in experiences, planned or unplanned, that have the potential to teach them how the world works and how to do things for themselves.

" "

Your child learns every day through real-life experiences, by watching you and others, helping with tasks, exploring ideas, and discovering new things.

LESSONS AWAY FROM THE CLASSROOM

It is important for parents to be aware that learning does not happen in the classroom only and that many key life lessons do not involve textbooks.

Your child learns from everyday life—through trial and error experiences, by exploring ideas, through independent discovery, by participating in tasks with others, or by observing others. You are constantly involved in helping your child learn—not only concepts and skills, but also to develop a lifelong love of learning. Memorizing the right answers helps them pass a test, but learning how to learn will get them through life.

Curious to learn

In a Montessori-inspired home, learning is viewed as a journey, not as a burden or a race. Some children do love competitive learning, but learning does not need to take place in a formal setting, with children competing for grades. Ideally, children learn because they are curious rather than as a response to external motivation or to prove that they can do something. As a parent, your goal is to consciously help your child not only develop basic skills that are taught in school, but also develop a love of learning and master practical, everyday living skills not taught in school. You can also promote cultural literacy on universal topics—in science, technology, invention, and medicine; in arts and literature; in health and wellness; and in current affairs.

Lessons at home happen naturally—at meals; at family meetings; and when talking, reading, and playing games. Often, the best way to help your child learn is to ask questions and listen rather than give answers. Learning should be a fundamental aspect of family life for all.

Embarking on projects with your child provides them with hands-on learning opportunities.

MAKING LEARNING FUN

We often struggle with the idea that learning can be fun—some of us may have negative recollections of learning experiences at school. However, we learn best when we have fun and enjoy ourselves. Children find learning fun when they are engaged. Thinking about a learning experience in your childhood that was enjoyable can help you find ways to ensure that learning is not difficult or boring for your child.

Ages and stages

18 months–6 years
Your child loves to do things with you. Helping you sweep, wash up, or prep food is joyful for them. Avoid flash cards, online learning, or textbooks—keep activities hands-on.

6–12 years
Help your child retain a sense of curiosity and enthusiasm. Follow their interests and keep absorbing books that reflect school topics. Watch short educational programs together, visit museums, and attend live performances. Keep learning experiential.

12–18 years
Help adolescents feel that learning makes sense, is exciting and satisfying, and can reveal interests and passions. Studying with friends, gently supervised, can satisfy their desire for social interaction while getting work done.

Individual learning pathways

Learning becomes natural and enjoyable when it is an experience that is free from embarrassment and intimidation. Sometimes children feel that they are not able to compete, whether with other children in the family or even with their parents. It is important to be aware that everyone learns things in their own way and at their own pace. It is also crucial to be mindful that on the path from being a beginner to mastering a task, mistakes can happen, whether playing a song on the piano or baking a cake. Children learn both from the things that turn out just right and, if they feel safe, from their mistakes. Natural consequences (see pp.82–85), assuming everyone is safe, allow your child to discover by doing.

Hands-on learning

Giving your child extra schoolwork to do at home to "reinforce" learning can backfire. Some parents find it comforting to have additional textbooks at home that their child spends time working on either on their own or with a parent. While some children may enjoy this, many do not. Instead, they learn to either tolerate the extra work as inevitable or they resist, often by letting their minds drift off, which leads parents to pester them. With a Montessori approach, parents are generally urged not to use textbooks or test papers at all,

" "

The home is a place where your child can explore and discover in a relaxed environment.

Activities such as making a favorite cake engage your child willingly in enjoyable learning tasks.

in particular with young children, unless they actually request them. Instead, parents are encouraged to think about their home as a place where children can explore and learn, having fun as they do so. Some children are happy to explore and discover on their own, while others like to watch someone doing something to see how it works before trying it for themselves. The following suggestions help make learning at home fun:

- **Making learning into a game** can be helpful for younger children. Games such as "I spy" help your child think about sounds and letters. Other observation games, such as seeing how often you can spot a certain word on street signs, build basic skills such as word recognition and counting.

- **As your child grows,** allow them to participate freely in everyday tasks so they learn by doing things with you. You can find opportunities for learning at home in a range of activities, from baking a cake to sorting socks or washing the car, to more ambitious projects such as building a birdhouse or renovating a piece of furniture.

STIMULATING YOUR CHILD'S MIND: YOUNG CHILDREN

The human brain is hardwired to respond to and learn from stimulation and interactions with the environment and other people. When your young child's developing mind is engaged appropriately, they not only grasp specific concepts and master skills, they also form neural pathways in the brain that facilitate their future learning.

Ideal learning moments

Young children pass through stages where they are particularly sensitive to certain kinds of learning. Some stages occur naturally without help from you, such as when your child learns to take their first steps, from which they go on to walk, run, and jump. Sensitive periods can also offer wonderful opportunities to stimulate your child's brain. During the first 6 years of life, your child learns through exposure and

Introducing experiences to your child, such as dancing, can ignite an interest.

66 99 OUR STORY

My son is 2 years old and fascinated by trucks. One day, he scribbled on his favorite toy truck with a brown marker. I walked into the room just as he was finishing. Looking pleased, he stood up and announced, "I will clean it now!" I immediately thought, "Oh no. This is going to be a disaster!" But I took a breath and decided not to interrupt.

He rushed to the bathroom for the foaming soap dispenser. He lathered his hands and rubbed the truck in a circular motion, then left to fetch a cup. I offered to help him move the truck to our front steps to avoid the inevitable mess, and he agreed. I then sat there as he poured water and marveled as it ran off the truck. He ran inside for a towel and dried every drop. I just gave him a few coaching words to help with the cleanup. He was beaming with pride as he negotiated whether to put away the soap or towel first and experienced the unparalleled feeling of independence at being the person to decide this, as well as at the feeling of satisfaction from the "big work" he had carried out.

Alicia (@montessibaby @teachlearnmontessori), mother of Charlie, age 2

their senses. For example, you can introduce a foreign language or music from birth by speaking the language or playing music in their presence. The connection between lived experience and your child's brain development means it is important to introduce stimulating activities and experiences consciously into family life.

- **Maria Montessori** used the metaphor of sowing seeds of interest and culture like wildflower seeds. You do not know which seeds of learning will germinate and thrive, but your child is likely to develop a sense of curiosity, creativity, wonder, and imagination.

- **Another lesson** from Montessori is to "follow the child." Pay attention to what they are drawn to and think of practical ways to help them develop an interest. Be mindful, too, not to pressure them to do things that they do not enjoy, as this may lead them to become resistant. Avoid overstimulating them, too. If they become irritable or distracted, let them pursue other activities of their choice.

STIMULATING YOUR CHILD'S MIND: OLDER CHILDREN

Children are naturally curious and, as they grow, continue to ask "what" and "why" questions, especially in the elementary school years. A fundamental way to stimulate their minds is to talk with one another constantly, as well as play games and share experiences.

Working out the answers

Your child knows that you have far more experience and knowledge than they do, so it is only natural that they will ask you for answers to their questions.

Conversing with grandparents and older relatives can give children a new perspective.

To keep their mind engaged and encourage their inquisitiveness, your goal is to help them learn that they can figure things out for themselves and to teach them that we continue to learn throughout our lives.

- **Think about how conversations** can help your child explore topics. For example, if your young child asks you why the sun looks so big at the end of the day, you may or may not know the answer, but you can use an online search engine together or show them how to look up information about the atmosphere in an encyclopedia. The search results will no doubt lead to videos and articles that will help both you and your child gain a better understanding of what is going on in the atmosphere. Your child sees that you are learning, too.

- **Talk about shared experiences**. Whether you are watching a television documentary, movie, or drama with your child; reading the same book; or have enjoyed an outing together, talk to them about it. For example, discuss what they found most interesting about a movie or book. Was there a character they particularly enjoyed watching, and how would they describe them to someone else?

Or, if you have been on an outing, what did they find the most interesting or enjoyable part of their trip?

- **Arranging conversations** between your child, yourself, and their grandparents or other older relatives can be an enjoyable and interesting way to stimulate your child's mind. You might consider recording the conversation for posterity. Children love to hear the stories that older family members have to tell. They can be fascinated by stories from grandparents about what it was like when they were growing up and how they came to live where they do. These stories not only carry on your family history, but they can also be intellectually stimulating. Do, however, watch out for signs that your child is no longer interested in a conversation.

- **Ask your child** to tell a story (if they enjoy this). Mastering the art of creating a tale or writing and acting out a short play can be extremely stimulating for children.

- **Introduce "heroes"** into your child's life. Is there a heroic character, either living or from the past, with whom they can identify and will find thought-provoking? This is especially important for families who are raising

" "

Talk to your child about your shared experiences—what did they like best about a movie, a book, or an outing you enjoyed together?

children who come from an ethnic or religious background that is a minority in their local community, because children need to feel connected to history.

- **As your child grows**, continue to provide games and suggest activities that engage their mind. Make sure that games evolve in line with their age. Think, too, about different types of activities, from ones they can enjoy on their own, such as building and construction blocks and jigsaw puzzles; to action games played with others; to advanced strategy games, such as chess or role-play. Older children can also enjoy teaching younger children skills and grandparents and parents how to keep up with technology.

INVESTIGATION AND DISCOVERY

Very young children ask questions to start a conversation rather than wanting to get a detailed explanation—they are simply exploring ideas. As your child grows, their exploration of topics of interest becomes more detailed and in depth, and the breadth of their interests is likely to widen.

Young explorers

Four- and 5-year-old children tend to learn through their senses while exploring anything that captures their interest. In a Montessori classroom, special learning materials help them do this while developing foundational skills in reading, writing, mathematics, measuring, organizing, and observing. Even though you may not have these learning materials at home, you can consciously help your child discover how to learn in a Montessori way.

For example, your young child may be interested in a butterfly in the garden. With your help and guidance, they can look through a book of butterflies from the library or in your home or search online to find out its name. Depending on their level of interest, they may be delighted with the information on how the caterpillar evolves into the butterfly,

how long it takes for that to happen, and what the caterpillar eats. After that, they may move on quickly to another interest. Or they might be interested in seeing what a chrysalis looks like. If you find a chrysalis attached to a branch, you could even bring this inside and put it in a terrarium or suitable container to allow the butterfly to emerge, which can be an unforgettable experience for a child.

Ages and stages

18 months–6 years
Allow your child to explore activities without your interference when they are engaged and focused. Observe them. If they become frustrated, watch for another minute or two to see if they can work something out. This helps them build perseverance and determination. Offer help if they are stuck.

6–12 years
Encourage your child to ask questions, read, and learn about whatever catches their interest. If you can, suggest they talk to someone you know who has professional insight into a field they enjoy.

12–18 years
Let your adolescent explore, investigate, and discover answers through research, travel, joining a debating team, or getting involved with a youth organization for a political party.

Close-up observation can be an engaging way for young children to investigate and learn.

Learning to combine skills

In the elementary school years, children are interested in the "how" and "why" and have vivid imaginations. They want to delve into subjects that catch their attention and are usually able to carry out simple research on their own to investigate and discover information through a process of asking a question and developing a theory, experimenting in some way to test the theory, or researching to discover the answer.

At home, investigation and discovery can be initiated by you or your child when questions are asked. Even though your child engages in more abstract thinking now, they still enjoy practical learning, and discoveries can involve combining reading, writing, and calculating with hands-on learning (see box, right).

Changing interests

In adolescence, children can start to focus more on relationships with peers, gender identity, sexuality, social justice, global situations, family values, and how they fit in and can make a difference. They may question why you support a political party and may want to gain a better understanding of the differences between organized religions. They may also be interested in ancestors: where they came from, what was going on in the world

when they were alive, and the impact world events had on them. Engaging in deep discussions, even if these lead to disagreements at times, helps your child explore and discover now.

Hands-on learning

Thinking about how you might approach a project, such as building a birdhouse, illustrates how you can help your child combine skills as they move through the elementary years.

The questions your child might need to ask could include: What type of bird is in your garden and what kind of bird would they like to attract? Does this kind of bird live in the area? How big are they, and what predators do they have? Work together with your child to find the answers, then start to design the house together. Choose the wood, work out the dimensions, saw and glue the pieces, and hang the birdhouse in a suitable spot. Finally, your child can wait for the birds to appear and record their observations.

GAMES AND ACTIVITIES TO STIMULATE THE MIND

Your child's brain develops through interacting with the environment. They learn by watching, hearing, thinking, and doing. As a parent, you can tailor activities to help your child develop their inner sense of order, concentration, problem-solving skills, language, and independence.

Learning through play

Many activities that entertain your child also help strengthen their problem-solving skills, develop their memory, and increase their knowledge. Watch your child to see how they engage with activities and try not to interrupt them when they are concentrating on something.

- **Children enjoy creating patterns**. Activities that involve sorting, nesting, and stacking, as well as recognizing the pattern in which blocks and objects can be arranged, engage sensory awareness and coordination.

Provide opportunities to recognize, repeat, or create patterns, for example, with beads, colored blocks in geometric shapes, or mosaics. You can also have fun creating patterns through movement, which builds memory and pattern recognition and develops coordination. Try performing a movement or dance step or clapping in a specific pattern or beat and ask your child to repeat your actions.

- **Touch recognition games** also develop sensory awareness. Place objects in a bag. Invite your child to put their hand in and determine what the object is simply by touching it.

- **Games involving puzzles** develop your child's problem-solving and math skills, as well as their

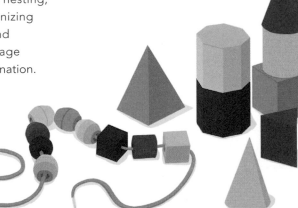

From building blocks to threading beads, children of different ages enjoy creating patterns with colors and shapes.

focus. These can range from first jigsaw puzzles, with just a few pieces and knobs to hold, to complex jigsaw puzzles for older children. Introduce abstract puzzle challenges, too, from simple "connect the dots" to crossword puzzles and word and number games.

- **Strategy games and activities**, such as tic tac toe, puzzle cubes, or board and card games, contribute to brain development by encouraging planning and logic skills and also teach your child to play by the rules. Games with dice help with number recognition and simple math.

- **Introduce activities** that build memory and observation skills. At around 3 years of age, show your child three or four objects. Ask them to close their eyes, remove one, then ask them which is missing. As they get older, use picture pair cards to test memory and focus. Or play a movie clip, then see if your child can recall details.

- **Story games** develop language skills, memory, and imagination. In the early years, play oral games where you take turns to add a sound, word, or sentence to create a story, challenging your child to remember and incorporate what the previous person said. As they grow, many children develop

---

Ages and stages

18 months–6 years
In the early years, activities that involve manipulating parts, such as building blocks, puzzles, or putting matching objects together, are key to stimulating your child's mind. Montessori said you cannot give anything to the mind without first giving it to the hand.

6–12 years
Many children continue to enjoy building with blocks or other materials, making models, or playing strategy games.

12–18 years
Teens enjoy playing games with friends. See if they are open to having friends over to join in a family activity. They may enjoy competing, as well as challenging board and video games.

---

vivid imaginations and enjoy creating and telling stories. Take turns to make up a story, then tell them in a way that makes them come alive. This stimulates the brain in ways that are different from listening to a story or reading. It also develops memory as your child keeps track of the story, its characters, the sequence of events, and what will happen next. Children who create and tell stories tend to have a stronger vocabulary and use of language.

ACTION GAMES AND ACTIVITIES

Games and activities at home that involve movement not only help ensure that your child gets valuable exercise and enjoys family time, but also develop coordination, strength, and agility, both physical and mental.

- **Many activities develop** your child's hand–eye coordination, important for everyday tasks and skills such as

Ages and stages

18 months–6 years
Young children learn as they move. At this developmental stage, they are working on coordination, strength, and agility. Simple games that involve movements such as running, jumping, hopping, and moving under and over things all contribute to the development of their confidence and grace.

6–12 years
Children often enjoy active outdoor games now, such as catching and other ball games and tag. They may also enjoy gentler activities, such as yoga and dance.

12–18 years
Teenagers are most likely to enjoy team sports. Many also enjoy running, cycling, or power walking with friends.

writing and drawing and helpful for participating in sports. Young children can start by gently tossing a bean bag into a basket from a few steps back. As their skill grows, you could create a slanted board with holes as targets so your child can play at a more advanced level. Other games that involve aiming for a target, such as croquet, or simple catch games with a ball also improve your child's hand–eye coordination.

- **Home obstacle courses** are enjoyed by children of many ages. These help children develop their balance and coordination, movement, visual perception, and problem-solving skills. Whether you set up an obstacle course indoors in your living room using chairs, pillows, boxes, and other suitable items or outside in your yard, aim to create a structure that involves your child climbing, crawling under objects, jumping, hopping, and walking.

- **Scavenger hunts** are great fun for children and allow them to be actively involved in reading a list, searching for items, and working as a team. The idea is that this is collaborative rather than competitive. Choose from a variety of themes, such as a hunt for

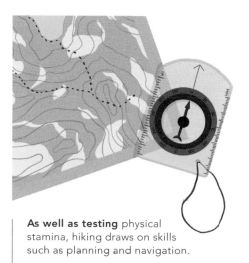

As well as testing physical stamina, hiking draws on skills such as planning and navigation.

children the opportunity to not only enjoy nature and get some exercise, but to also learn how to follow a map and/or pay attention to the landmarks you pass along the way. With older children, hikes can last for hours or maybe even overnight. Hikes can be especially valuable if you involve your child in thinking about what you need to bring, from snacks and water to a first-aid kit, extra socks, rain gear, or a compass. They can help gather the items and pack a backpack.

items around the home or for nature items in the garden or local park, then make a list of items for the hunt. Smaller children can team up with an older sibling or parent; older children might work individually or in a team. Give your child or team a certain amount of time to find the items listed. At the end of the hunt, gather around and share the items you have found.

- **Hiking** is a valuable experience for children of any age. Children need to spend time outdoors and benefit greatly from the companionship of family walks. Longer hikes offer

- **Some families enjoy** practicing yoga together, whether with an instructor, from a video, or by preparing yoga "posture" cards for their children to try. Yoga not only leads to good balance, flexibility, strength, and inner calm, it also contributes to children's brain development, coordination, and "body mapping"— the self-awareness of our bodies in relation to our surroundings.

- **A dance-off** can be fun for the entire family. This develops your child's coordination and helps them enjoy movement. Try dancing to energetic music in an informal competition, either together or individually, where you dance until one of you is declared the winner by mutual consent.

SHARING BOOKS

Reading together is one of the best ways for families to stimulate their minds and feel closer to each other. If you enjoy reading and integrate it into family life, your child is likely to enjoy the benefits of sharing books and reading throughout their life.

Introducing books

No child is too young to enjoy snuggling with a parent or older sibling as they are read a story. When choosing books for your toddler, bear in mind that they are developing their visual sense, so large

illustrations with minimal text is ideal. As your toddler learns vocabulary, point to pictures and name them, then to the word describing the picture, drawing your finger across it as you say the word. As their vocabulary grows, progress to picture books with sentences.

Montessori teaches children the sounds of letters before their names so they learn to read phonetically. Say the sounds when pointing to a letter. For example, for the letter "s," say "sssssss" instead of "esss."

Young readers

Many children start to read on their own, or with help, around the age of 5. Offer books with exciting vocabulary and captivating content. Keep the following in mind when selecting books for children aged 18 months to 6 years:

- **Very young children** cannot easily distinguish between fantasy and reality. Their understanding of the world is based on what they can touch, smell, see, hear, and taste. Look for books with fairly realistic illustrations instead of books that show animal characters acting and dressing like people, which give

Sharing books with a looked-up-to older sibling can be a magical experience for a young child.

children a false impression of how real animals behave. While some classic books do this, try to stick to books with realistic stories and illustrations.

- **Rhyming stories** are fun and natural for children. Rhyme and repetition also help them remember stories. Young children may repeat learned words and sentences while looking at a book before they know how to read.

- **When your child** is around 4 years old, read short chapter books to them a chapter at a time, as well as picture books. Talk about the characters, the story, and how they felt about a chapter.

Broadening horizons

In the elementary years, children move into a period of imagination and creativity, making up their own stories. Read books to them now that are several levels above their own. They also want to know the how and why. Encourage them to use libraries—at home, in school, or public ones—as well as online sources to gather information from encyclopedias, dictionaries, and other nonfiction sources.

For reluctant readers, comics, magazines, and audio books can help develop an interest in reading.

In adolescence, your child becomes more interested in relationships with others and enjoys books and stories that explore moral or social situations.

Ages and stages

18 months–6 years
For toddlers, choose board books with real-life photos or drawings, without words near the picture, or with an explanatory word on a separate page. Young children love books that rhyme. Encourage your child to join in with rhyming words or repeated phrases. Form a habit of reading regularly with your child, not just at bedtime.

6–12 years
Try starting a family book club, where you ask open-ended questions to help your child formulate and express ideas.

12–18 years
Adolescents may start to read a diverse range of material. As well as fiction, they may increasingly read nonfiction—such as biographies, autobiographies, and topical books—for pleasure. Help them access more diverse reading material.

Looking after books

When you begin reading with your child, as well as teaching them about words and stories, you are also showing them how to handle books carefully, turning the pages gently.

Show your child that care must be taken not to step on books; that they should not be thrown; and that, like other objects, they need to be put away when finished.

ENJOYING ART

As well as being part of our history and a way of understanding other people's experiences, art is also a form of personal expression, like poetry, song, dance, and telling stories. It is a form of human connection that can evoke feelings, thoughts, and hopefully appreciation and understanding. Montessori encourages families to expose children to as many forms of art as possible.

Ages and stages

18 months–6 years
From painting with water on smooth stone to using paints, clay, or crayons, children can explore color and different media now, developing hand–eye coordination and expression. Visit a gallery if they enjoy this.

6–12 years
Some children may continue to enjoy creating art and appreciating others' art. Encourage them to frame and display their favorite work. Continue to invite them to visit galleries with you.

12–18 years
An interest in art may be rediscovered now, providing adolescents with a vehicle for self-expression and creativity that helps them clarify their identity. Students may explore digital art and photography.

Introducing your child to art

Exposing children to art and crafts—together with music, dance, movies, and theater—and surrounding them with art in our homes helps them have a sense of the vibrant texture of the world and our common history. When your child is young, display art from your family's culture and from other cultures and familiarize them with well-known artists from around the world.

A creative environment

Artistic creativity is one of the many ways that children can express their personalities and intelligence. As well as being an expression of personal experience, it also plays a key role in developing learning, problem-solving abilities, and planning skills. Encouraging the artistic side of your child's personality can pay dividends for life.

- **Set up a prepared environment** that encourages creativity. This space could include media such as paints, collage materials, pastels or charcoal, or sculpting clay, depending on changing interests. For a young child, start with a small table and chair, if possible, with paper and some type of storage facility or drawers where they can put crayons, markers, small pompoms, feathers, and other things that could be used for craft projects.

> 66 99
>
> Encouraging your child's interest in art and giving them room to be creative provides them with experiences that will endure.

Letting your child explore art from an early age fosters creativity and aids motor development.

- **Young children** start off by using their hands to create finger paintings or drawings in a tray of sand. They need plenty of practice to develop the muscles in their hands and fingers and coordinate their movements before using tools such as pencils, crayons, or paintbrushes. They usually love the process of creating and are less concerned with how the art looks. However, they feel pride when their art is displayed at home. Plan how to display and share their favorite work.

- **School-aged children** may develop an interest in a particular art form or media. This might signal a shift in their attention, from simply exploring and working with media to being more focused on a finished product.

They may enjoy finding objects to use in nature or from a garage sale as their imagination and creativity blossom. Peer interaction is also important now. They might wish to join an art class with their peers or integrate an art activity into their birthday celebration.

- **If your child joins an art class**, help them explore themes. Discuss the lesson with them and, if they are interested, visit a museum or watch a movie about a particular artist together. Encourage them to source library books or online material that illustrates a style they are interested in, such as still life, or discusses an artist whose work centers around the style. They could also set up a still-life arrangement to practice at home.

LEARNING ABOUT MONEY MANAGEMENT

A long-term goal in Montessori-inspired homes is to teach children about money and the part it plays in our lives. Learning to manage money involves developing a wide range of everyday skills and helping children grow up with a balanced set of values on money, possessions, savings, investments, charitable giving, and debt.

Ages and stages

18 months–6 years
Giving a small allowance starting around the age of 4 can help you guide your child into thoughtful habits around using money.

6–12 years
Adjust your child's allowance to reflect the items they will need to buy. Learning to live within an allowance is a key skill. If they spend it too quickly, let the natural consequence of not having enough teach them to be more conscious of spending in the future.

12–18 years
By adolescence, your child has hopefully learned to be careful with money. You may need to increase their allowance so they can save for bigger purchases, helping them learn more about planning ahead and avoiding impulse buys.

Setting an example

Helping your child understand and use money wisely is one of the steps to them becoming independent, resilient, responsible, and innovative planners, decision makers, and problem solvers. Children absorb life lessons about money from observing how their parents spend it, share it, and save it. These lessons begin as your child watches you use money, for example, as you pay for things at a store.

How you talk about money influences your child's ideas about abundance or scarcity and models money decision-making behavior. For example, hearing thoughtful discussions about expenses, budgeting, and investments teaches your child the importance of talking about finances. Even if you do not directly involve them, your child sees, hears, and senses these patterns in your life.

You can also help school-aged children become financially literate by explaining the difference between an asset, which appreciates in value (and, ideally, brings some income), and a liability, which depreciates in value and costs money to own. Your child can learn that things that we need, such as a home or possibly a car, cost us money to maintain, and that understanding the costs involved is important to a family's decision-making process.

The benefits of an allowance

Giving your child an allowance from 4 to 5 years old helps them start to think about money management. Talk to them about having their own money and how they can spend it wisely, use it for a worthy cause, or save it. Show an older child how to create a written budget using their allowance as their income to determine expenses and plan savings. From an early age, help them think about making good spending choices. They should consider the need versus the desire (see below), the value versus the cost, and the total amount that they have available to spend. These valuable steps help them manage and track money independently and responsibly.

Wanting and needing

Be thoughtful before buying something just because your child wants it. Help them distinguish between things they need, such as equipment for a class they have enrolled in, and things they want, such as a new toy. Save the latter for special occasions or, even better, help them learn save and maybe earn extra money so that, in time, they can buy it themselves.

Find practical ways to teach your child to avoid impulse buys. You could plan a meal together. Compile a grocery list and shop for the food together, buying only the items on the list. Ask them to add up prices as you go along. This teaches them how to choose between brands, stick to a list, and keep track of expenditure.

Sticking to a planned list while shopping with your child teaches them a valuable life lesson.

Teaching your child the fundamentals of savings and investments helps prepare them for the future.

Building on an allowance

As your child grows, they may want to buy more expensive items and their allowance, even with savings put aside, may not be enough. This can be a chance for you to help them explore ways to earn additional income. They might do jobs around the house above and beyond their usual tasks, as well as for other people. Also, with or without your help, they might look at ideas for starting a small business of some sort, whether running a lemonade stand, helping out in a family business, or starting a small business of their own. This sort of venture helps your child become innovative, independent, and responsible while earning extra money.

Keeping balances in check

Once your child has learned the basic principles of budgeting, help them develop this practical life skill, showing them how to ensure bills get paid, look at cash flow projection, and reconcile expenditure and balances.

- **Whether you have** paper bank statements or bank online, talk to your child about the different ways to make payments and how to check these against your statement at the end of the month to be sure that the figures match. If you have home accounting software, show your child how this works for setting up accounts, entering incoming bills, and planning what needs to be paid and when.

- **Older children can learn** how to keep track of their expenses, read a bank statement, or use spreadsheet software to develop a monthly budget and compare actual expenses against their budget. They can project how well they are working toward long-term saving or investment goals.

Credit and savings

Using credit wisely is another important lesson for your child. Ideally, large items are paid for fully upfront. If you need to finance something over time, teach your child how to look for the best terms and to factor ongoing costs into their budget.

It is a good idea to make savings a deliberate part of your child's money

" " **OUR STORY**

My 7-year-old grandson wanted a mountain bike so that he could join his older brother, who had a mountain bike of his own, on rides through the nearby park.

His mom and I talked about the possibility of getting him one as a birthday present, but we felt that he was now old enough to contribute to its cost. Together, we proposed that she and I would each cover a third of the cost, and he could earn his share by walking the family dog and giving it its weekly bath for two months. He earned his share, week by week, and took special pride when it was time to go to a bike shop and pick out his own bike.

David, grandfather of Asher, age 7

planning. Some families simply regard savings as a family expense, while others view them as an opportunity to teach children to save for large purchases, unexpected trips or activities, or emergencies. How much your child saves now is not significant, but the lessons they learn from this are valuable.

" "

As your child gets older, they will become more involved in managing their own money and can start to plan for their future.

Planning ahead

Your child will become increasingly involved in managing their money and future plans. Show them how to plan by working together on a "family strategic plan." This includes what the family wants, what you need to do to get it, who will be involved, and how long it will take to achieve. It could include future plans for your teenager, such as the costs of further education, starting a business, or travel. Help them look at ways to create money through investments, whether they partner in a business venture, develop a source of passive earnings, or learn about the stock market. Choosing companies to invest in gives them the chance to explore if there are some whose mission and practices better reflect their personal values.

HOMEWORK

Too often, homework is a battleground between parents and children. Regular homework is not part of Montessori schooling, but for families where schools do set homework, there are ways for parents to make it a positive learning experience rather than a struggle.

The Montessori approach

In Montessori, traditional homework is not the norm. Instead, "school work" done at home is usually an outgrowth of what children are interested in, whether that is reading; making a presentation; planning and budgeting family meals; or writing invitations, letters, emails, or an article. There may be a test to study for or a project or research to do, but most academic work is done during school hours, with at-home projects used to put children's knowledge or skills to practical use. Home time is for absorbing, reflecting on, and internalizing information learned at school.

"Family learning time"

Whatever your child's homework regime, the Montessori ethos can help families set up a basic routine to make work that is done during home time more pleasant for everyone. Before a school year starts, discuss "family learning time" at a family meeting. Think about when and where this will happen, what type of activities each of you will do, and how it will help. Agree on and stick to a time and place for the whole family to engage in a learning activity—whether reading, doing online research, or working on the measurements and design for a model. By preparing for this time and letting everyone express their thoughts, you reinforce the idea that each member of the family is a lifelong learner, that learning is enjoyable, and that it is important to be present so that each of you can work individually or ask for help.

- At weekly family meetings, let each person share what they have coming up that week. One parent might be preparing a work presentation, a child might have a test to study for, another may have chapters of a book to read and report on, and the other parent

Being mindful of your message

Keep in mind that your own approach to work sets an example for your child. If you talk about your work negatively and approach it as a chore, you signal to your child that work is not enjoyable and is something that simply has to be endured, in contrast to relaxing leisure time. Conversely, expressing the satisfaction you take from your work shows your child that work can be a fulfilling endeavor that forms an integral part of life.

may be doing genealogy research. This conversation means each family member knows what's coming up and makes it easier for everyone to understand and support each other.

- At the start of daily family learning time, check in with your child. What do they need to achieve? Share what you hope to accomplish. This will help your child structure their learning time and set them up for success.

Ages and stages

18 months–6 years
Read, read, read; count everything; match and sort. Create and act out a skit and sing and dance together!

6–12 years
Help your child be organized. Help them manage large projects, but don't do them. Ask about work, but don't say how to do it.

12–18 years
Ensure your child has the support for more advanced assignments. This gives them the sense that if they need extra guidance or time you are there, but that they are able.

Quietly sharing a space while each family member enjoys learning time creates a focused and mutually supportive homework environment.

Show an interest in your child's work, but encourage them to find their own solutions.

" "

With the right approach and encouragement, children will explore and learn about whatever captures their attention.

the ability to apply skills and knowledge in new situations. Moreover, when parents and teachers use rewards and pressure to try to get children to work, children can end up resistant and resentful of lessons, teachers, homework, and tests. Test anxiety is a major concern. Many parents want to help children not only succeed, but also excel, and feel they need to give them an external push.

Why children learn

The purpose of education is not only to pass tests, but also to become a well-informed and thoughtful member of the adult community and someone who can adapt to an ever-changing world.

Children are usually born intelligent, curious, and creative. When given the chance, they will explore whatever captures their attention without needing encouragement or external structure.

There is growing concern that often schoolwork is oriented to memorization more than understanding in context or

Your role as a parent

As well as providing the structure and support discussed on pages 138–139, consider the following when thinking about how to help your child manage and enjoy homework.

- **Pay attention** to how much work they have. Does it seem interesting or mundane. How much time do they need to spend on it? Do they seem to be coping or seem stressed, resentful, or exhausted? If they are working until late at night or seem anxious, respectfully talk to their teacher, who can identify if your child is being given too much work and/or needs additional support.

- **Avoid the temptation** to add after-school academic enrichment or support unless you have a good reason to believe your child needs it, or they ask for it and find it enjoyable.

- **Learning should be interesting** and enjoyable, not something dreaded and resented. Many parents feel they need to spend time doing extra work with their child. This is great if you both

enjoy it but is a very bad idea if either of you gets frustrated and discouraged.

- **Treat your child's homework** as their task. If they ask for help, ask them to explain what they have in mind and how they aim to achieve it. This helps them understand what needs to be done and how to get organized. Do not take over partially or completely. Projects are given so that students learn by doing something and demonstrate understanding through completing them (see also p.142). If you do the thinking, your child will not learn.

66 99 OUR STORY

When my son Joseph reached middle school, he often struggled to complete homework on time. He was unprepared, uncooperative, and full of excuses. Reasoning didn't work, so we decided to talk about it at our weekly family meeting rather than try to deal with it in the heat of the moment. The calm nature of weekly meetings made it possible to express our concern and commitment to helping him succeed.

I asked Joseph whether there was anything that we could do to help him get his work done other than doing it for him. He described feeling overwhelmed at all the things he had

to do and saw his tendency to get bogged down. We agreed to try to help him list and prioritize work and to think about what he would need to do to accomplish each piece. He had always been an active child, so we suggested that he complete a task, put it in his bag, then do some push-ups or other physical activity as a "brain break." For him, this worked. He would periodically ask for help, and I would check in with him to see how he was doing, offer words of encouragement about his effort and progress, and congratulate him when the day's tasks were done.

Daniel, father of Joseph, now age 15

HELPING WITH PROJECTS

Your school-aged child will periodically have more substantial homework projects—such as learning lines, making a model, or setting up an experiment—which require preparation over days, weeks, or longer. Your role is to support them in developing the planning and organizational skills required.

Ages and stages

18 months–6 years
At around age 4 or 5, your child may announce that it is their turn to "show and tell," or that they need to learn the lines of a song. Encourage them, give choices, and help them take the lead confidently.

6–12 years
For longer projects, avoid last-minute scrambles, taking the lead, or doing too much for them. As well as helping them think through the project and note each step as it is completed, commend them along the way for their effort and progress.

12–18 years
Children can face more and increasingly complex projects. Ask questions to help them focus their efforts on what is due, when, what steps are involved, and how they can manage it with minimal stress. Encourage rather than rescue them.

How you can assist
The aim is to help your child learn how to think through and carry out a larger project by coaching and inspiring them but never doing the work for them. Instead, ask questions and help them organize their thoughts if needed.

An organized approach
Weekly family meetings are an ideal time to keep abreast of more involved school commitments. As each family member shares what is coming up over the weeks ahead, you can note major projects or events in your diary. If your child mentions a school project, set up a time to discuss its details and to offer your support. This helps avoid the frustration and stress of learning about important plans at the last minute.

You can guide your child and support and encourage the completion of their project by helping them develop skills steadily, learn how to organize their thoughts, prepare a timeline and plan the steps, and think through what materials and resources they will need.

Practical help
The range of projects can vary widely depending on the age of your child, the approach of their school, and the subject matter. Do not expect perfection. Instead, help your child feel comfortable doing the project

" "

Asking your child questions and helping them organize their thoughts supports your child and encourages them to think for themselves.

themselves and try to improve with each new assignment. There are a number of ways to support them.

- **If your child is preparing** an oral or written report on a book or a class presentation, for example, about a historical figure or event, help them find ways to add interest. They could prepare a PowerPoint presentation, use props, or dress up as a character.

- **Brainstorm ideas** for science projects together. Coach your child in the planning: how they will conduct the experiment, how they will display the research and results, and how they will explain it to others.

- **If your child is memorizing lines** for a play or class reading, offer to listen as they practice. Gently coach them on how to dramatize the message and prompt them to think about how well they are doing. For example, after listening, ask how they felt about it.

What did they think went well, and what might they do differently? This approach keeps them from feeling they are not good enough. You could also offer to record them. Encourage them to watch and critique themselves. If you have a knack for drama and your child does not feel uncomfortable, you could show them how you might do it. Be mindful that they only have so much emotional energy to work on a project like this at any one time.

- **Encourage them** to help prepare any costume or props. This will help them feel that they have been involved in every aspect of an endeavor.

Suggesting creative ways to engage in a project, such as dressing up, can help your child find new ways to explore topics.

SPENDING TIME TOGETHER

It is easy to be part of the same family, living in the same home, and yet spend relatively little quality time with one another.

Spending time together is important for every member of the family. If you have a partner, spend time with each other in meaningful communication and nurture your relationship. However your family unit is made up, the goal in a Montessori home is to nurture a family that is close, cooperative, and mutually supportive. It is also important to be mindful that, while your family has an identity of its own, it is made up of unique individuals, each with their own interests and distinct personalities. Forging a family is about creating a small community of individuals— of parents, children, and sometimes extended family, all living together.

" "

The time that you spend together in mutually enjoyable activities helps strengthen family bonds and individual relationships.

NURTURING YOUR FAMILY

Spending quality time together is important for strengthening family relationships. There are many ways to build this together time into family life, from the routine of everyday life to enjoying outings and planned trips together.

Being together

Each day, we have opportunities to connect with each other: at mealtimes, on the way to school, or relaxing in the evening. Beyond these everyday routines, building in time together—playing, learning, traveling, reading, and sharing stories—helps build the family unit. Creating and sharing memories and traditions is also important. These become part of the ongoing story that your child will pass on to their own family when asked about their childhood. You also nurture your family when you enjoy projects and activities together, such as embarking on a small building project.

It is important, too, to set aside your digital devices so you focus on each other. Disconnecting from the digital world and our separate activities is vital to enable us to reconnect with each other and put our relationships foremost.

Setting aside time to enjoy activities as a family helps build and nurture each relationship.

SHARING FAMILY STORIES

Family stories are usually shared spontaneously and informally in everyday family life. Children can benefit in big and small ways from knowing more about the lives of the people in their families, both those who are alive now and from stories about their ancestors.

Opportunities for family stories

Being open to the many chances that arise in family life to share and pass down family stories can help your child feel a sense of belonging. These family stories can bring up emotions for the people involved—of humor, sadness, appreciation, or love. Sharing stories with your child and displaying emotions helps your child explore their own emotions.

You may find stories are sparked by your child asking about your childhood, or when asking their grandparents about what it was like when they were growing up. Stories may also come up at family gatherings when someone is reminiscing, or when visiting a place where you lived or visited frequently as a child.

- **Family stories can provide** an opportunity for humor. They are often comical and funny, and your child will love enjoying the merriment and

laughter they create. Do be careful to ensure that the humor you enjoy does not include sarcasm or making fun of other family members, but rather that it teaches your child that an optimistic view of situations helps families build resilience and healthy attitudes, no matter what comes along in life. Demonstrating this gentle family humor teaches your child how shared stories can generate laughter and a feeling of warmth that everyone can enjoy.

Ages and stages

18 months–6 years
Your young child loves to hear you tell stories about your family and will often ask you to tell stories again and again. Other family members may chime in as stories are retold and become part of the fabric of family life.

6–12 years
Your child may be eagerly interested in delving deeper now, talking with grandparents and other relatives about their childhood experiences, going through photo albums, and even doing online family research.

12–18 years
Teenagers may lose interest in family history for a time, or interest may grow. They may want to create their own family history, collecting photos and recording interviews with family members to make an oral history.

" "

Telling family stories
when opportunities present
themselves gives your child
a strong sense of belonging.

Weave in stories about family
and ancestors when looking at
photographs to help your child
feel a sense of shared history.

- **Family stories** can hold valuable
  lessons for children about topics such
  as bravery, getting through hard
  times, and standing up for family
  beliefs, or about practical matters
  such as starting a business.

Bringing ancestors to life

When stories have been told over several
generations, find ways to help make
them more real for your child. If you have
old photographs of the people in the
story, show these to your child. Visiting a
grave to put down some flowers can also
bring up memories and stories.

During the elementary and adolescent
years, your child may become more
interested in who their ancestors were,
especially if they can link them to a topic
they are studying in history. For example,
they may be intrigued by the women's
fight for the right to vote, where a
great-great-grandmother may have been
part of the movement, or how their
great-grandparents' life was affected by
war. Sharing stories about them can help
make that part of history come alive. If
ancestors migrated, children can learn
about the part of the world they were
born in and what life was like there.

MAKING AGREEMENTS

Disagreements are part of everyday life. Resolving conflict and making agreements with your child after a dispute is important for them to learn about their relationships with siblings, parents, friends, or other relatives and live peacefully together.

When children disagree with each other, parents act as facilitators to help them think through what happened and how they can resolve conflict (see pp.108–111).

Similarly, when you and your child disagree, the Montessori approach is for you as the parent to engage with them so that you can resolve the conflict and reach an agreement. Whether your child bothers you to buy something; fails to do a chore; or, as a teenager, spends money unwisely, your role is to model peaceful conflict resolution skills.

If emotions are running high after a disagreement with your child, it can be best to disengage and take a break before trying to resolve things. Wait for a neutral moment, when you are both calm, before discussing it. It is vital as a parent to stay calm and somewhat detached to avoid being defensive. It is also important to separate the "deed" from the "doer" so your child knows that, no matter what they say or do, you love them. The strategy on pages 150–151 showcases how to reach an agreement peacefully.

" "

Waiting for a quiet, calm moment to discuss disputes can help you and your child to reach agreements amicably.

66 99 OUR STORY

Our youngest child is still at home, while our two older children are at college. After some time, she began to feel lonely without her older brother and sister around. So she did something she does not often do: she asked for something—she began asking us for a dog.

My wife and I were concerned that she would quickly tire of the responsibilities of having a pet. So we began to prep her for ownership of a dog by carefully explaining all of the work and obligation that would follow. Her desire for a dog was not thwarted. We then made an agreement that she would be completely responsible for its care.

The day we brought home the puppy, she took to him immediately, naming him Ollie. From day one, she exceeded our expectations for how she would care and attend to the puppy in every single area. As with most 14-year-old children, the reality for Mattison was the hard work of being responsible for caring for another life. We do help from time to time, but we do not take over. We let her go through it without bailing her out, without being a crutch, without allowing her to abdicate the responsibility that she asked for, and she has grown a great deal in light of it. No matter the situation, she does what she has to do to make Ollie's existence a good one.

Michael, father of Isaiah, age 23, Morgan, age 22, and Mattison, age 14

MAKING AGREEMENTS IN PRACTICE

Wait for a calm moment

If, for example, you are drawn into an argument with your child when you are out shopping together because you have said you will not buy something that they want, try to stick to your guns but resist getting drawn into a big dispute in the store. Instead, wait until you get home and are both feeling calmer, then revisit what happened at the store. You might say to your child, "We need to talk about what happened when we were at the store today."

Acknowledge their feelings

Begin by letting your child know that both of you played a part in the problem. You might say something like, "I know that we both argued about what to buy when we were at the store. I don't like to argue and make a scene in a store, and I'm pretty sure you don't like that either. Am I right?" This not only lets your child know that both of you have some responsibility in continuing to argue in the store, but it also lets them know that you care about their feelings.

Talking together calmly after a dispute can help you and your child avoid a similar situation in the future.

Reach an agreement

Once you have acknowledged what happened and have made it clear that you both had a part to play, invite your child to help you think of some ways to resolve the situation and keep it from happening again. For example, you might decide to not shop together if it is not necessary, to leave a store if an argument starts, or to use an agreed-upon signal to stop if an argument begins. Once you have talked through your ideas, choose one that you both agree on and try it out.

66 99

Agreeing that you both played a part in a disagreement helps your child understand that you are seeing both sides.

Choose future consequences

If your child does not follow through with an agreement, talk again. You might make a new agreement with consequences that you work out together. If a situation affects the whole family, you could discuss it at a family meeting. The point of a consequence is not to punish your child, but to teach them. You are helping them stop behaving inappropriately, understand your concern, and behave responsibly. When choosing a consequence, ask yourself the following:

Have you ensured that the chosen consequence relates to the situation?

Is this consequence a reasonable expectation for your child?

Does the consequence show respect to your child and the family?

Will the consequence help your child take responsibility?

PLAYING TOGETHER

Competition is often used in schools, in children's sports, and by adults to externally motivate children into an artificial spirit of competition. In contrast, Montessori encourages a spirit of friendly, cooperative work and play that can appear very different from the typical competitive mindset that many cultures take for granted.

A different approach

Many think that a Montessori philosophy does not recognize competition. Montessori does appreciate that many situations involve competition—at school, at work, and in the home—and sees this as a natural part of life, where sometimes we win and other times we do not. However, Montessori nurtures a spirit of cooperation and collaboration rather than promoting the sense that life is a competition for attention or a prize.

Often, visitors to a Montessori classroom are surprised to see children of different ages getting along so well. The wonderful spirit of collaboration and sharing that is promoted allows children to work and play together or beside each other, enjoying both the experience of shared time and the celebration of each other's unique achievements and milestones. Children help each other be successful. There is an absence of oneupmanship, and children appreciate each other's accomplishments.

A spirit of cooperation

In Montessori-inspired homes, parents celebrate each family member as unique, with their own gifts, challenges, and rates of progress. They recognize and appreciate each person and what they have accomplished on a task and encourage other family members to acknowledge and appreciate other's accomplishments and achievements at family meetings and in everyday life.

Ages and stages

18 months–6 years
Model sharing and cooperating for your 2- to 3-year-old and help them use words to express needs. From 3 to 5 years, they are ready to learn about sharing.

6–12 years
Learning a new sport or skill during these years can be frustrating for your child. Helping them be comfortable with the journey of learning and the idea that this may include losing from time to time teaches them an important life lesson.

12–18 years
These years can be challenging, as teens may pull away or be frustrated with younger siblings. Find ways to keep them connected to the family and also welcome their friends.

Learning to share

In the first six years of life, children are learning how to be in relationships. In their first two to three years, dependent on their parents for their care, they tend to think the world revolves around them.

Between 2 and 3 years of age, they begin to realize that they are separate from their caregivers—they can do things on their own and can express their needs verbally. As they become increasingly capable, act as a guide and mentor, helping them cooperate and become aware of others' needs.

At this age, children find it hard to share toys and their parents' attention. Some parents try to persuade children to share. Do not force sharing now. Your child prefers to play on their own, with others close by, and is just learning what sharing means. They do not understand the difference between sharing a toy for a time and giving it away forever. Help older siblings understand this. You could suggest older children play with something else for a little while. With children over 3 years old, facilitate a conflict resolution scenario if a squabble over sharing arises (see pp.108–111).

At 3 to 5 years of age, children start to master turn-taking. Show them how to share respectfully, guiding them through situations and modeling appropriate behavior.

Enjoying competitive play

Through the elementary school years and adolescence, children often enjoy competing and are more focused on outcomes. Help them recognize that learning a new concept or skill is a process that involves mistakes. Show that playing together—whether a ball game, a board game, or charades—is something we choose to do voluntarily because we enjoy it. This helps children compete in a way that is healthy for their relationships.

Mutually enjoyable activities help children have fun participating and competing without feeling pressured to succeed.

153

FAMILY PROJECTS

Getting involved in a family project gives you and your child an opportunity to plan and work together and brings a sense of accomplishment. Ideally, such projects bring you closer and leave your child feeling that it was an enjoyable experience and that they also gained practical life skills.

Working together

Whether your family project is a large job that needs to be done in or around the house or something you are making for your child to enjoy, the idea of working together is the real goal. Obviously, the practicality of the entire family working together depends on your own skills and the age of your children.

- Projects that could involve the whole family range from assembling a new bed or item of furniture for your child's bedroom to building a deck where the family can enjoy meals and spend time together outside.

- Creating a play area for your child, such as a sandpit; setting up outdoor play equipment; painting a small play table indoors; or even the construction of a treehouse can be something that the family undertakes together.

- A family project outside of the home could involve some sort of community service project. You might volunteer for a worthy cause, such as delivering meals or preparing food packages for needy families or helping out at a food bank, or work together, for example, to help clean up a public park or riverbank.

Willing helpers

When you embark on a family project with your child, it is important to consider how they feel. Do you think they feel coerced into helping and possibly resentful, or do you think they are feeling that spending family time working together on something beyond their routine household chores is a positive experience?

As a parent, your aim is to help your child understand that each family member does need to help out in some way and that at times we do not always

Ages and stages

18 months–6 years
Your toddler may be aware that a project is underway. By 3 to 4 years, a child can have some supervised involvement. By 5 to 6, they can handle child-sized tools and work independently on some parts of a project.

6–12 years
Your child may suggest a project or make a meaningful contribution to the planning process. They can learn a lot by helping. Find jobs they can do safely according to their age, strength, and maturity.

12–18 years
Adolescents should be able to plan, organize, and complete many projects on their own or with some support. They can play a full role, planning and using tools correctly.

Collaborative projects teach your child about teamwork and completing tasks.

have a choice. To work in harmony on family projects, it is important to minimize stress and to disarm any squabbles that arise among family members as calmly as possible. This helps your child come away from early experiences feeling positive about the time they spent working together or helping with a chore.

Realistic expectations

Be careful not to set unrealistic expectations for how long or how hard your child will work on a project and be practical about how much help they can give you at a certain age. Appreciate that their ability to maintain focus and

interest on a particular task and their level of commitment to completing a project are likely to differ from yours. The goal of embarking on family projects together is not simply to get the job done, it is to lead your child to understand that there are times when everyone needs to pitch in and that this is a normal and positive part of family life. Ideally, your child will come away from a completed project with a sense that this was something you achieved by working together. Over time, they may develop a sense of shared responsibility and pride and accomplishment when a project is carried out successfully.

EVERYDAY STRATEGIES
A QUIET SPACE

We all experience emotions such as frustration, anger, disappointment, or loneliness. How we express these at times can be hurtful or damaging. In Montessori, all emotions are seen as part of life. We want to help children recognize emotions, self-calm, and learn to express how they feel.

When your child is young, often their first instinct when upset is to cry, hit, or throw something. You can begin to help them recognize and identify feelings, giving them new vocabulary to start to express themselves with words rather than behavior. Simply telling them to calm down is unlikely to work and can trigger fresh upset because they have not been taught how to do this. Instead, you could say, "I can tell that you are upset/angry. Breathing deeply and slowly can help. Let's try it together."

Once you have introduced the idea of emotions to your child, at a family meeting, discuss creating a "quiet space" for each family member (see pp.158–159). This is a comfortable place where they can go when upset to calm down, coming back to the family when they feel better and are ready to interact appropriately.

The goal is not to punish, but to teach—the true meaning of discipline (see p.40). Your child begins to learn about emotions, how these affect behavior, and how to behave more appropriately in the future.

66 99

A quiet space helps your child think about their emotions and begin to see how these can affect their behavior.

66 99 **OUR STORY**

When our children were about 4 and 7 years old, we started to discuss the idea of creating a quiet place for each family member. When they were younger, we tried to help them put words to their emotions so that they could calmly express how they were feeling. Still, sometimes there were outbursts for one reason or another, so we thought quiet places might give each of us a place to go to calm down and feel centered.

Both Clark, the eldest, and Natalie were very enthusiastic about the idea of a quiet place. Clark wondered if his quiet place could be outside, dribbling and shooting his basketball into the hoop in our driveway. Natalie wanted to have an area in her bedroom for artwork and a cozy space where she could snuggle up with her stuffed toy animals. I chose my small computer room where my music could be played, and my wife chose her rocking chair in our bedroom.

Although we weren't certain at first whether this strategy would work, we found that each person's idea worked for them. Our quiet spaces definitely helped when one of us needed some time alone to regroup. We still use those spaces today.

Robert and Ruth, parents of Clark, age 14, and Natalie, age 11

A QUIET SPACE IN PRACTICE

Talk about privacy

At the family meeting, discuss how each person's quiet space is a private place where they can be alone and calm down. It is the opposite of "time out," used by parents as a last resort and which can make children resentful and unlikely to reflect on behavior.

Make it a joint decision

Work with your child to decide where their quiet space will be. Involving them in the decision helps them feel that this is their chosen space and is most likely to lead to their cooperation and willingness to embrace the concept of a quiet, self-calming space.

A tool for all

Agree on a guideline that anyone in the family can suggest to another family member that it might be helpful for them to take a quiet break. Discuss this at the family meeting, when everyone is calm and there is a feeling of being part of a team.

Agree to accept suggestions

Make an agreement that each family member will listen to and cooperate with a parent's or sibling's suggestion to take a quiet break. If someone agrees to this at the meeting but does not carry through when a situation arises, try the strategies, opposite.

Create your quiet spaces

Discuss each person's space. Some find activity calming. The "what and where" could be a cozy corner; a rocking chair; playing a ball game; or being in the yards or a workshop. There might be books, cushions, or music and headphones; a fish tank; paints or clay; or even a miniature Zen garden.

Avoid time limits

Do not set a time limit on the person taking a break. In contrast to "time out," a self-quieting space is designed to help your child self-regulate: to know when they are upset and need a break, to take time to think about a problem, and to know when they are calm enough to rejoin the family.

When your child says "no"

If your child says "no" in words or actions when you ask them to visit their quiet space, try the following:

Bear in mind they may think it is a punishment, especially if an older child has experienced "time out" before. You may need to stay with them the first few times to let them know that this is a comforting place. Once they settle in leave them so they can experience self-calming on their own.

Be the model for your child. Go to your quiet place. Use strategies such as deep breathing or reading. Say, "I feel better now" on your return.

As a last resort, ask if they need your help going to their quiet place. If so, lovingly guide or carry them there.

" "

A quiet space provides a place where family members can think about a situation and regain a sense of calmness.

A comfortable self-quieting space encourages self-reflection and helps to promote self-regulation.

ENJOYING NATURE TOGETHER

Montessori values include caring for and preserving our natural resources and the planet and placing an emphasis on families spending time in nature. Being in nature together enhances relationships and helps your child develop a strong sense of connection to the natural world. This might even lead to them becoming involved in the protection of the natural environment.

Observing nature

Studies show that children who connect with nature seem to be calmer and more grounded than those who spend more time indoors, often on digital devices. As a family, spending time in nature—whether gardening, walking in the park, hiking in woods, or consciously observing nature up close in any or all of these settings—is enjoyable, affordable, and good for the physical and mental health of all.

Spending time together in natural environments engenders a connection to and respect for nature.

- **Equip your child** with tools such as a magnifying glass, a bug box or jar, and a small guidebook to help them collect and identify items you find on nature excursions. If you have space at home, you and your child could create a nature area to display your finds.

- **Help your young child** notice plants and animals at different stages of development. They can use their magnifying glass to observe objects such as eggs, possibly taking photos of them before they hatch. Teach them the important lesson of not disturbing natural processes and letting creatures exist in their natural setting.

- **Help your child** become a detailed nature observer. Suggest they choose a place to sit, in your garden or other natural environment, and spend five minutes really looking closely at this spot. After five minutes, they can talk about, write, or draw what they noticed. Ask them questions about what they observed, such as, "What colors did you see in the grass? Did you see any insects? What sounds did you hear?"

- **Your older child** might like to keep a nature journal. This could be a written or photographic record, or you could encourage them to draw plants from nature, which might lead them to

Ages and stages

18 months–6 years
This is a crucial time in your child's development for connecting with nature. Spend as much time as possible outdoors playing, exploring, eating, and relaxing to help your child develop a deep sense of being part of the natural world.

6–12 years
Longer, more involved activities—such as staying up late to star gaze, hiking, and fishing—stimulate the mind now, as well as exercise the body and help families bond.

12–18 years
Teenagers may enjoy joining the family in activities such as jogging, cycling, camping, and canoeing. They may like to draw from nature and practice nature photography.

develop an interest in botanical illustration. Drawing from nature will help them notice small details that they might otherwise miss. You could create a digital journal together, with video clips of the passage of time, possibly recording something you both planted while it grows.

- **Encourage your child** to write poems and stories that capture the sense of wonder in nature.

OUT AND ABOUT: YOUNG CHILDREN

Whether going to the store, to the park, or on a longer outing, going out with children aged 18 months to 6 years involves ensuring you have everything you need to care for them away from home. With some thoughtful planning, this challenge becomes manageable.

Your child's needs

In Montessori-inspired homes, parents consciously show respect, empathy, understanding, and consideration for their children from birth onward. This means planning ahead before leaving the house to make outings as comfortable and pleasant as possible for everyone. Whether your child adapts easily to changes in their routine or struggles to cope with disruption, show them respect and consideration before leaving the house. Ask yourself why you are going out and whose needs will the trip meet: yours, your child's, or both of yours? Once you have decided on a trip, taking into account all your child's needs—during the journey and for clothing and food throughout your trip—will help you plan. When you are out, being aware of the signs that your child is tired and irritable will also ensure that you are thinking of their needs.

A little independence

When toddlers and young children are engaged in play dates with friends at the park or spend time at a playground, they begin to move away from their parents slightly as they play. Naturally, you will stay close by to keep an eye on them, and they will return to you every so often to make sure that you are still there, but this activity means they are starting to experience a degree of independence. These are times when you can teach your child to stay within sight, to hold hands when crossing streets, and to take turns.

Thinking about stamina

When planning a family outing with your young child, bear in mind that, as well as being costly, large amusement parks or

When children are bored

Parents often worry about children being bored, for example, if an outing is not stimulating enough.

Encouraging your child from as young as 2 years of age to be creative and think for themselves means they will rarely be bored because they will learn how to find things to do, to build, or to discover for themselves. Conversely, when constantly entertained and engaged, they can feel at a loss if left to their own devices.

❝ ❞ OUR STORY

Whether I'm heading out with my toddler for a few hours or for an entire day, I always try to prepare to ensure as smooth an outing as possible. For us, this looks like packing up some engaging activities for the inevitably long car ride—such as various books, mess-free art options, and anything that involves magnets—and a healthy snack or a picnic lunch.

I also make sure that I have all of the necessary clothing items, including extras, depending on the weather and our destination of choice. Knowing I have an extra outfit in the car allows me the mental ease of letting go of any worries I may have of them getting dirty, and I am able to let her explore her surroundings freely, which almost always includes getting wet and muddy!

Most importantly, I plan for plenty of time at the destination of choice. Allowing for ample time once we arrive takes away any unnecessary pressure of time constraints and gives her the respect and freedom to explore to her heart's content.

Lauren (@modernmontimama), mother of A, age 2 and K, newborn

Being prepared before heading out with your young child demonstrates your consideration of their needs.

events with long lines and crowds of people can often end up being a stressful experience for younger children. This type of trip is better suited for older children who have more stamina and independence. When planning outings with your young child, opt for simpler, smaller activities without too many distractions. These activities can often provide fun learning experiences and, ideally, there will be plenty of space to move around in and relax.

OUT AND ABOUT: OLDER CHILDREN

When deciding on outings with elementary school–aged children and adolescents, planning ahead is key to ensure that everyone is happy and to avoid power struggles or exhausted children having a meltdown. Your goal is to enjoy positive experiences that form lasting and loving memories.

Routine outings

Routine shopping trips or similar outings may be unavoidable with your child. However, many children do not enjoy shopping, unless it is to buy something that they want, and it is common for parents and children to feel frustrated.

If your child feels involved in a shopping trip, they are likely to be more engaged, which will set both you and your child up for a more enjoyable experience. You could talk to them about what needs to be accomplished, and they could help prepare a shopping list. On a supermarket trip, ask an elementary school–aged child to lead the way to different parts of the store. Although you want them to stay close to you, you can help them feel as though they are playing an important part by guiding the cart carefully around other shoppers.

With an older child, consider a strategy for dividing up the shopping, maybe putting them in charge of finding certain items on the list while you shop in another section.

Identifying shared interests

Family meetings (see pp.22–23 and 64–67) are the best place for families to explore what they wish to do during the week.

Use your weekly family meeting to list all the activities that members of your family currently enjoy doing together. The concept of doing things together that you all wish to do—rather than doing something that an individual is interested in—is crucial to ensure that everyone has a positive experience.

Bear in mind, too, that some family members like to set plans far in advance, while others might prefer to be more spontaneous. Being aware of these different preferences can help you balance each others' needs.

> " "
>
> When your child feels involved in an outing, whether a routine shopping trip or a planned activity, they are more likely to be actively engaged.

Planned trips

Recreational activities are a chance to enjoy time together in new environments. You can expose your child to activities that involve being with others, as well as experiences that require you to stay together and take care of each other.

- **Bear in mind that long journeys** can be challenging, so think carefully before routinely taking children on a long road trip. If you do need to travel far, try to turn the journey into a family bonding experience by singing together, conversing, playing games, telling stories, or listening to an audio book that everyone enjoys. Ideally, avoid downloading movies and programs onto devices that your child watches on their own. While this may stop them from becoming irritable, it means that family members are in their own worlds rather than bonding with each other.

- **Help your child learn** how to enjoy experiences and notice what is going on. Find activities that the whole family will enjoy. This might be going on a hike on the weekend or enjoying hobbies together such as cycling, canoeing or kayaking, or fishing, where you can enjoy nature and get some exercise. You might take binoculars to look for birds and wildlife together. Outings that involve visiting local fairs, farmers' markets, or a festival can open up new worlds to your child while also helping them learn life skills, such as moving calmly through a crowd.

The time spent getting to a destination provides a perfect opportunity to chat together without distractions.

SPECIAL OUTINGS

Enjoy outings with your child that are outside of your everyday norm, such as visiting a restaurant, museum, or public event. These outings expose them to experiences that you feel are an important part of growing up, where they can learn about the community and culture in which they live and may develop an interest in new activities, places, or ideas. You can also teach them how to behave politely, appropriately, and safely in a particular situation.

Ages and stages

18 months–6 years
Choose outings carefully now to minimize disruption to routines and keep your child from becoming overstimulated. Pack activities such as coloring books. Be ready to leave if they show signs of being tired.

6–12 years
Guide your child on how to behave in an audience or at a restaurant, how to stay safe at a public event, and how to manage on long journeys. Include them in planning snacks and activities.

12–18 years
Your teen should be quite independent when choosing clothing and packing for outings. Check on their plan without micromanaging.

What to consider
When choosing a special outing for the family, take into account the age of your child and their readiness. From an early age, you can begin to teach your child how to be well behaved and considerate of others in a new situation. However, consider whether it is reasonable to ask your child to participate in a particular event or outing where you can predict they are likely to lose interest quickly or where you think they will lack stamina. For example, is your very young child likely to become restless and behave inappropriately in a restaurant?

Introducing new experiences
Special outings can help your child develop new skills and an appreciation and understanding of a variety of experiences. You can help them learn to stretch their interests and begin to be aware of and appreciate new activities when you introduce them in the right way.

- **Before going out**, let your child know what the outing will involve, how you expect them to behave, and the appropriate clothing for the outing.

- **When you introduce** your child to a new situation, it is wise to expose them only briefly at first. If, for example, they have to sit through a long play or an entire sporting event, this can leave them feeling tired

Introducing your child to new experiences, such as visiting a gallery, broadens their horizons.

and grumpy and also feeling reluctant to repeat the experience. Your aim is for them to think of the outing as a positive experience.

Choosing outings

Think about experiences that you believe will be exciting, affordable, and practical for your family, whether in your local community, a day trip close by, or as a vacation. Ideally, a family outing or vacation will help your child become aware of the things your community and beyond have to offer. This could be a new type of cuisine, an exhibit at a local gallery, a play the whole family might enjoy, or new landscapes.

It is important to include older children, in particular, in planning during family meetings, as they will have their own ideas. You could give them an open-ended choice, discussing timings, costs, and points of interest. Or suggest two or three possibilities that you have considered in advance. This ensures that they are aware that you are considering a particular trip; helps them get some idea of what the experience might be like; and, hopefully, makes them feel that they were part of the decision-making process.

REFOCUSING MISBEHAVIOR

No matter how many preventative strategies you put into place and how much you read up on parenting, your child will at times misbehave. They are in the process of trying to manage emotions, express their needs appropriately, and understand their boundaries and limits.

Your response to your child's behavior can have a positive or negative effect on how they learn communication skills, resolve problems, and take responsibility for actions. Parental responses that uphold Montessori values include remaining calm when interacting with your child, recognizing that they are learning, avoiding taking their behavior personally, and helping them work through concerns. There are many reasons why a child's behavior may be challenging, disruptive, or aggressive. Irritability and being out of sorts can be due to hunger, tiredness, feeling unwell, or sensitivity to changes. Being aware of your child's physical needs and thinking ahead help. Behavioral issues also arise when your child is trying to convey their emotional needs—to feel loved, to have control, to belong, and to feel valued (see p.38) The strategies on pages 170–171 will help you deal with challenging behavior that arises from these needs.

"

Your child is learning to express their needs appropriately and to understand their boundaries and limits.

66 99 OUR STORY

We noticed that our 8-year-old daughter seemed to whine and fuss or simply disappear when it was time to do the least little thing, from getting her own breakfast, to making her bed, to choosing her clothes for an outing. We knew that she was perfectly capable of doing these everyday tasks on her own, but … it just wasn't happening.

So I decided to break down the tasks into smaller steps that she could succeed at and build up her self-confidence. However, that didn't work, and things seemed to get even worse. She became sadder and disappeared to her room more frequently. Finally, after looking for patterns and deciding that it wasn't a simple matter of, for example, her being tired or trying to test limits, it dawned on me to check my own feelings when situations came up. When I began to pay attention to how I felt instead of just noticing my daughter's actions, I realized I was feeling annoyed. I was then able to look beyond my annoyance and see that what she really wanted was my attention.

She and I talked about how she was feeling and how she could talk to me about her thoughts, then we came up with some ideas to help her feel that she was loved and important. She asked if I could join her in cleaning her room sometimes. She also asked if we could have some snuggle and reading-together time before we turned the lights out at bedtime. It was amazing how easy it was to meet her needs when I realized what the whining and fussing were all about.

Jane, mother of Cheryl, age 8

REFOCUSING MISBEHAVIOR IN PRACTICE

A need to feel loved

If a child constantly seeks attention, even when you are busy, they need to be reassured that you love them. Notice when they approach. Without talking, reach out with a loving gesture to signal to them to come closer. Do not halt your task. This simple action can help to avoid their behavior escalating.

A need to feel some control

If your child challenges your authority— for example, refusing to do a task— they need to feel that they can make decisions. If a dispute is important, at a calm time, invite them to talk. Say you know that they feel nagged, but a solution needs to be found. Work on one together, and stick gently to this.

A need to belong

If your child is unkind to you or others, they need assurance that you accept them, if not the behavior, and that they are integral to the family. For example, a child may feel left out when a new baby arrives and say they hate them. Try saying, "I understand how you feel; the baby takes up my time, I'm sorry. Let's find ways to spend time together."

A positive gesture can reassure a child that they are loved, while you also signal that you have an important task to do.

A need to feel valued

If your child seems discouraged, they may need reassurance that they are capable. Break tasks down into steps. Encourage them to do the first step. Acknowledge this when it is done. You might finish the task, then next time encourage them to add a step so they build on small successes.

Dealing with power struggles

As well as talking to find a solution when your child challenges you (see opposite), there are some additional ways to deal with power struggles:

Give choices. These can be narrow choices—for example, deciding between two types of clothing.

Let go of your position. Sometimes we find it hard to listen to our child's ideas. Children can be very creative and may find a different solution that achieves the same goal. Be prepared to listen to their solutions.

Put them in charge. For example, if you are having a battle about a task, putting them in charge gives them a sense of leadership.

Use one word on tasks that you have already agreed they will do. For example, about loading the dishwasher, simply say "dishes."

Agree a signal. If power struggles are frequent, find a signal that you can both use if you feel one starting to remind you both to stop and start again.

THE BIRTH OF A CHILD

When a child is born, whether a first child or a sibling, it changes the family dynamic. Preparing for your baby's arrival involves practical considerations, such as reviewing the space in your home and the supplies that you will need, as well as preparing older siblings to welcome the new baby and working with your partner.

Being prepared

Think about the space available for sleeping, playing, changing, clothing, and feeding. If your new baby will need to share a bedroom with a sibling, talk to your older child about this to prepare them for their new roommate.

This is also the time for first-time parents to discuss parenting practices, discipline, and family values (see pp.20–21).

New family dynamics

With your new baby's arrival, much of the family focus will be on interacting with and caring for them. Nurture relationships during these years, spending time with your partner and sharing caregiving. A new baby can have a dramatic effect on older siblings, who can wonder where they fit into the family and feel that the new baby receives everyone's attention. Your goal is to help them feel a sense

66 99

A baby's arrival can shift focus in a family, and siblings may need guidance to feel a sense of connection.

Showing your child how to handle and care for the baby, with your supervision, helps them embrace their new sibling.

66 99 OUR STORY

As any new parent, the birth of our first child brought feelings I had never felt or experienced before. With the waves of emotion, I felt like a fuller person. I was proud, happy, and in love with my daughter and had dreams for her future. I also became more fearful and anxious for her and the world she was brought into.

When my wife was expecting our second child, our daughter fell in love with my wife's growing tummy. She listened, watched, and touched. We told her how her brother was growing. The day of the arrival came, and I took her to her favorite store to pick out a special present for her brother. We did this for our third child, and in both cases the siblings were welcomed with complete joy. For the announcement of our fourth child, my wife came home with balloons and a cake. Two of our children celebrated. The other one broke down in tears and with great sadness cried out, "Another one!" Fast-forward four years, and our four children are with each other seven days a week and live in love and peace ... mostly.

David, father of Eden, age 10, Eli, age 8, Ewan, age 6, and Ethan, age 4

of family connection—that there is enough love for everyone and that they can play a key role as the older sibling. Before the birth, discuss what will happen, answer questions about how things will change, and reassure them that each family member is important. A child may hear these words and not take them seriously and may feel left out or resentful. Look for signs that they feel this way, listen if they voice concerns, and answer questions honestly to minimize worries or fears.

- **Invite siblings** to join in with welcoming the baby. They can help prepare their room or pick out books for them.

- **After the birth**, depending on their age and interest, siblings can help bathe, feed, or read to the baby.

WHEN FAMILIES CHANGE

When families evolve and grow through adoption or fostering, or when two people with children from previous relationships become partners and form a blended family, often a number of new relationships between adults and children need to be forged and well-established routines adjusted.

Family structures

Each family is unique, and families have many different faces. The strategies and guidelines discussed throughout this book apply to all family structures. In a home inspired by the Montessori ethos, the aim is to create an environment where children and other family members can grow and develop deep

" "

Whatever the make-up of your family, the aim of parents is to create a home where family members can develop deep bonds with each other.

bonds with each other. Hopefully, these bonds are profoundly positive, kind, mutually supportive, and filled with love and respect.

When households change, new relationships may need to be formed, for example, between older children and adults previously unknown to each other. Additional time and care may need to be taken to ensure that each person feels loved, heard, and that they belong, and also to help new family members learn to live together in harmony.

Challenges for families

When a new adult or adults come into a child's life, there are often many fresh challenges for the child to face.

With blended families, a child may have already been through the trauma of separation, divorce, or a parent dying. They face additional challenges when a new adult partners with their parent and becomes part of the child's life. It can be awkward or difficult for a child to accept, and hopefully come to love, a new parent figure. Children may also need to adjust to new siblings, whether these are the children of a parent's new partner, or children are joined together in families through adoption or fostering.

Some children can find this an incredibly joyful experience. Other children may feel sad, afraid, resentful, or confused. The process of helping

Creating a welcoming environment for a child helps ease the transition into their new home.

children adjust to each situation requires a lot of patience, love, and everyday parenting skills.

- **If you are in a couple**, work closely to form a united parenting team. Try to understand what each child is going through and present a warm, loving, and consistent set of guidelines as the new family dynamic evolves. With blended families, respect for all the members of all the families involved is sometimes the most challenging and the most important lesson for both children and adults to learn.

- **If older children**, originally from different households, are becoming part of the same household, allow the children time to get to know each other so they can settle in gradually to their new, expanded family. Give each family member in the household time to bond before taking a vacation or introducing a new family member to people in your extended family.

- **If you choose to foster or adopt**, involve any children of your own in the process. Talk to your children at a family meeting about what this means and how it could affect your family life.

- **Be patient**, kind, and consistent in helping new children understand and become accustomed to a family culture and house rules (see pages 22 and 41) that may be different from the ones they are used to.

GUIDING SIBLINGS

The family is a safe place for siblings to learn to communicate, collaborate, share, and disagree, secure in their love for each other. As parents, our goal is to guide siblings through their interactions with each other and help them develop the skills needed to create rich and loving relationships inside and outside of the family.

Respecting relationships

Each child is a unique human being, and their relationship with a sibling may not be as you imagined it, or how you experienced sibling relationships as a child. Different personalities and interests, as well as age differences between siblings can sometimes cause children either to be very close and share many interests or to prefer to engage in their own activities.

Patterns of behavior

Falling-outs between siblings are common in families and, ultimately, you may have to get involved to help sort out disagreements. Whether one child is trying to get their sibling into trouble or is trying to get your attention, patterns of behavior can develop. Watch for these patterns at different stages as your children grow. Try to stay calm and observe what is going on objectively and use strategies to short-circuit behavior before it gets started or goes too far. Try the strategies on pages 108–111 to disarm squabbles; pages 156–159 for quiet, self-calming spaces; and pages 168–171 for refocusing common misbehaviors.

A secure sense of belonging

Your goal is to try to ensure that each child feels that they belong, that they are seen for who they are, that they are loved and respected, and that their voice matters.

- Teach your child that, while their voice is heard, they need to respect others and to not be mean or hurtful.
- Help your children learn how to see, listen, and appreciate one another and how to support each member of the family.

Dealing with disagreements

Sibling rivalry is common in many families and can be challenging for all. This may take the form of a child vying for your attention by doing something that they believe will make you proud or elicit praise, but that actually creates disharmony within the family, or that tests your family's house rules (see p.41). Help your children understand that there are consistent, fair, loving, and firm limits for behavior within the family.

Using the weekly family meeting to discuss disagreements and come up with solutions, spending some private time with an individual child having a quiet conversation about squabbles with siblings, or engaging in a pleasant activity with the whole family helps siblings learn how to get along and resolve their disagreements.

- **Help siblings enjoy** family activities harmoniously by giving each child the opportunity to lead and helping older children recognize that younger siblings are learning about turn-taking.

- **Be aware** of how you respond to your children. Try to put judgments aside; focus on facts rather than emotions; and stay calm, firm, and consistent.

❝ ❞

Siblings sometimes have squabbles, but the family is a safe place for them to learn to communicate with each other.

Ensuring that children feel listened to and can see that family rules are applied fairly helps siblings co-exist peacefully.

FAMILY TRADITIONS AND CELEBRATIONS

The traditions and celebrations that families enjoy create comforting patterns during the childhood years and help parents underscore the message that their children are loved and cherished.

Celebrating the traditions passed down to us from our parents, possibly creating a few new ones, and discovering the traditions of our own and other cultures and faiths opens us to the wonder and delight of life. Certain celebrations, whether or not we formally belong to an organized faith, can also help us teach our children in simple ways the moral and spiritual lessons of love, kindness, joy, and confidence in the fundamental goodness of life. Creating everyday routines that celebrate family life also fosters a sense of safety and security.

66 99

Enjoying celebrations together and following and creating family traditions nurture your child's sense of joy and appreciation of life.

A SENSE OF WONDER

One of the most precious gifts that we can give our children, through celebrations and family traditions, is an education of the heart, nurturing their sense of joy and appreciation of life, providing a sense of the poetic, and connecting them to humanity.

Passing on traditions

Family life is often hectic and stressful and, all too soon, children shift their focus from family to friends.

- **Activities and events** such as birthdays or a trip or vacation that you enjoy on an annual or regular basis, possibly involving the whole family, are a chance to spend time together and to reconnect with our sense of curiosity and joy.

- **Family traditions** and celebrations can also help us reconnect with nature. Children can help us get back in touch with the beauty of the world as we gather shells, shout into the wind, fly a kite, or leave a trail of footprints in the sand. Being alive to the beauty of our world and the seasons nurtures a spirit of inner peace and reverence for life. Without a sense of wonder, the world becomes commonplace; however, when we open ourselves to a sense of wonder, our souls can stir.

Customs such as annual vacations that strengthen bonds and create precious memories are deeply reassuring.

EVERYDAY TRADITIONS IN FAMILY LIFE

Family traditions can be both large and small. As well as annual festivities, acts of kindness and celebration can be woven into everyday family life. These small, thoughtful acts and activities enrich your child's world. Children will often remember, cherish, and pass on some of the day-to-day family rituals that you create and share.

Expressing gratitude

Creating traditions that help family members express their thanks to each other regularly is an important part of family life. As well as starting family meetings with a moment to appreciate and acknowledge what family members may have done (see p.22 and p.66), you can also create simple, everyday ways for family members to record acknowledgments and express their thanks to each other. By helping children to recognize the importance of expressing gratitude, we teach them social skills and help them to build strong relationships.

- A "thank you" board in the kitchen, or simply a piece of paper displayed on the fridge, can be a place for family members to say thank you to each other.

- A "kindness" wreath can be a fun way to express thanks. Each time someone notices a kindness, they add a ribbon to a wire frame, creating a colorful wreath.

- In your child's early years, slipping a note into their lunchbox can mean a great deal to them. You could leave a humorous, caring message or maybe just a few words of love and encouragement.

Simple, loving gestures can create a tradition that your child carries forward through their life.

Creating memories

Everyday traditions can also be created around mealtimes and at other moments when the family is all together. At meals, maybe on weekends, adorning the table with candles, flowers, and special dishes can add a touch of festivity, and thanks and gratitude can also be expressed now (see p.80).

After dinner, you could set aside time every now and then for a family literature activity. The idea of this tradition is to create a positive experience and fond memories and teach your child about enjoying non-screen-based activities that include interaction with others and foster a love of literature. This might be just half an hour where you read aloud to one another, maybe a poem or extract from a book, and share cherished tales before getting on with other activities such as hobbies, homework, or watching television.

This can encourage your child to think about and discuss a story or book that touches on emotions or sparks the imagination. When your child is old enough to read, if they wish, they can take a turn to read aloud. The experience should be fun and not a burden, so gauge if this is something they are happy to do.

Ages and stages

18 months–6 years
Establish a tradition of calling the family to dinner. You could sing a song, ring a bell, or quietly go around and invite each person to the table. At the table, you might have a tradition of saying a prayer of thanks or reading a poem before you start to eat.

6–12 years
At bedtime, ask your child what was the worst and best thing about their day, what made them laugh, and what they learned.

12–18 years
As you would with a younger child, check in with your teenager in the evening. Reflect with them on their day and share something about your day.

" "

Small, everyday acts of kindness and celebration can become a part of your family life, creating traditions that your child may continue.

CELEBRATING THE SEASONS

Seasons mark the passing of time in our natural world. In many families, there may be traditions that are shared throughout the wider culture, and, of course, your family can create seasonal traditions of their own.

Observing the seasons

Whether seasonal changes are distinct or there is little difference from one season to the next, no matter where you live, there are seasonal changes. Days grow longer or shorter, animals migrate to or from a region, plants flower and fruits ripen, wildlife offspring are born, or the weather may be drier or more rainy. Observing seasons teaches your child about the natural changes that occur over the year. Draw their attention to small details that they might overlook.

Marking the seasons

There are many ways that people celebrate the solstices, when we pass from one season to the next. Your family might choose to celebrate the beginning of a new season by placing something that is symbolic or representative of the season either indoors or outside. These actions help young children sense the passage of time and the continuity of the seasons. Your child can enjoy learning about why the items that you have chosen to bring into your home or to decorate your home with are connected to the seasons.

While the seasons may look different in each part of the world and the traditions that are celebrated where you live may be different from elsewhere, there will almost certainly be common ways in which the passage of time is marked and the seasons celebrated. These rituals will normally involve decorations, foods, activities, and traditional events.

Ages and stages

18 months–6 years
Draw your child's attention to visible signs of a change of season, such as the first spring buds, and talk about the seasonal equinox. At around 4 to 5 years, recruit your child to help with seasonal decorations.

6–12 years
Your child takes great pleasure in helping with seasonal decor or projects. Help them understand the symbolism behind traditions.

12–18 years
Help your child recognize that they will be able to carry on seasonal traditions. Gently encourage them to participate or take the lead in traditions.

A seasonal nature table develops your child's awareness of the patterns of nature where you live.

- **Think of ways** to signal the seasons. In northern hemispheres, a pumpkin or a wreath with colorful vines, leaves, nuts, and berries can signify fall, while holly and evergreen branches announce winter. In subtropical areas, palm fronds may be gathered. A display of seasonal flowers or a basket filled with seasonal produce also celebrate the seasons.

- **Young children enjoy** thinking about and remembering things that are typically associated with the seasons. For example, winter coats, raking leaves, sledding, and cooking traditional dishes and hearty soups are associated with colder months.

- **Children love to gather** items that represent the seasons and special holidays. Keep some of them from year to year. Pack them away and joyfully take them out as part of your annual traditions. Other annual family traditions might include forcing bulbs to flower inside in spring, filling vases with branches from flowering trees or bushes, or growing tiny meadows of grass in baskets filled with potting soil.

CELEBRATORY FAMILY GATHERINGS

Many family gatherings center around the life cycle of the family, with families gathering to celebrate or commemorate significant life events, depending on a family's beliefs, customs, and cultural traditions.

Celebrating anniversaries

Wedding anniversaries, birthdays, the anniversary of a death, cultural or national holidays, or annual reunions are all times when families gather to celebrate their connection and reminisce.

Ages and stages

18 months–6 years
Try not to go overboard with birthdays. Create a tradition of celebrating your child's growth, keeping it simple, focusing on them, and letting family members share their love and appreciation for a child's unique qualities.

6–12 years
Help your child appreciate what an occasion is about rather than think of it solely as a time to collect gifts.

12–18 years
Major rites of passage mark the transition to adulthood now. Help your child focus on the symbolism of an occasion and on the dignity and importance of the milestone.

Wedding anniversaries are a chance to share photos and videos with your child. You can recount your special day and establish the idea of a family history.

Birthdays are particularly special for your child, because they honor the start of their life and their awareness of time and history through their personal story. As well as a cake, gifts, and a birthday song, there are plenty of ways you can choose to mark this day.

- **Try introducing the idea** of the cycle and length of time that it takes the earth to rotate around the sun. Invite guests to sit in a circle. Place a candle in the middle to represent the sun and give your child a globe to represent the Earth. Say that it takes one year for the Earth to revolve around the sun, and that, since the day your child was born, it has traveled around the sun a set amount of times—the age of your child. While your child carries the globe slowly around the circle for each year of their life, recount a brief story and share photos from each year.

- **Light a special candle**. Gather around it and ask your child to share the most significant events of the last year and their dreams for the coming one. Express your hopes for them for the year ahead.

- **Every year**, add items to a time capsule for your child. Seal it and put it away, to be opened on their twenty-first birthday. Include photos, artifacts, and a letter from you reminiscing about milestones and events. Your child can look forward to opening this cache of treasured memories.

Rites of passage

Formal rites of passage occasions, such as baptisms, graduations, weddings, or funerals, may involve your child sitting through a ceremony or attending an animated party that may overwhelm them.

Be respectful of your child and give thought to how they might participate, if at all. Avoid asking them to carry out a role that they will struggle with. Think about whether a young child will be able to behave appropriately in an audience, congregation, or celebration and how you can help them have a positive experience that does not disturb others.

Balance finding ways for them to participate and form memories and bonds with being sensitive to what they can cope with. For example, you might arrange for them to attend just for a short time to form a special memory.

Gathering to celebrate an anniversary gives families a sense of belonging, togetherness, and shared love.

INDEX

REFERENCES

Page 100, Bedtime: Older Children
"Adolescent changes in homeostatic and circadian regulation of sleep," *Developmental Neuroscience*, 2017, DOI: 10.1159/000216538

FURTHER READING

The Discovery of the Child, Maria Montessori, The Clio Series, Vol. 2, 1997

The Child in the Family, Maria Montessori, Montessori-Pierson Publishing Company, 2007

Montessori from the Start, Paula Polk Lillard and Lynn Lillard Jessen, Schocken Books (a division of Random House Books, Inc.), 2003

Montessori for a Better World, Aline D. Wolf, Parent Child Press (a division of Montessori Services), 2017

How to Raise an Amazing Child: The Montessori Way (2nd edition), Tim Seldin, DK Publishing, 2017

ACKNOWLEDGMENTS

The authors would like to thank their families for their patience and support now and over the years. They are definitely the "wind beneath our wings." We also appreciate our many friends and colleagues who offer advice and counsel, which have been invaluable during our careers.

Dorling Kindersley would like to thank the following for their contributions:

Alicia Diaz-David @montessibaby @teachlearnmontessori

Chaneen Saliee @chaneensaliee

Carine Robin @montessorifamilyuk

Lauren Weber @modernmontimama

Claire Wedderburn-Maxwell for proofreading and Vanessa Bird for indexing.

ABOUT THE AUTHORS

Tim Seldin is the President of the Montessori Foundation and Chair of the International Montessori Council. During his more than 40 years of experience in Montessori education, Tim served as a Montessori guide as Headmaster of the Barrie School in Silver Spring, Maryland (which was his own alma mater from age 2 through to high school graduation), and as Executive Director of the NewGate School in Sarasota, Florida.

Tim was the co-founder and Director of the Institute for Advanced Montessori Studies and the Center for Guided Montessori Studies. He earned a BA in History and Philosophy from Georgetown University, an MEd in Educational Administration and Supervision from The American University, and his Montessori certification from the American Montessori Society. Tim is the author of several books on Montessori education, including *How to Raise An Amazing Child*; *Building a World-class Montessori School*; *The Montessori Way* with Dr. Paul Epstein; *Finding the Perfect Match—Recruit and Retain Your Ideal Enrollment*; *Master Teachers—Model Programs*; *Starting a New Montessori School*; *Celebrations of Life*; and *The World in the Palm of Her Hand*.

Tim is the father and stepfather of five former Montessori students and grandfather of a new generation of Montessori students. He lives on a small vineyard north of Sarasota, Florida, with his wife, Joyce St. Giermaine, and their horses, dogs, and cats.

Lorna McGrath is the Director of the Montessori Family Alliance, a division of the Montessori Foundation, and host of the Montessori Family Life Webinar Series.

During her career in education, she has taught in Montessori classrooms for 3- to 6-year-olds, as well as in the public sector for middle and high school students. She spent many years as the Associate Head of NewGate School in Sarasota, Florida, and is a member of its Board of Trustees. She is an adult educator in several Montessori Teacher Education Centers in the US and China. She received her BS in Home Economics Education and her MEd with a concentration in Family Counseling, and holds an an American Montessori Society teacher's credential. She is a trained parenting instructor and is the creator of *The Parenting Puzzle: The Basics*, a course that helps align home practices with Montessori values and principles.

Lorna and her husband, Larry, enjoy interacting with their adult children, who grew up in Montessori schools. They are especially thrilled that their grandson attends a Montessori school now. In her spare time, Lorna loves gardening, making quilts and other sewing projects, and traveling with Larry.

Project Editor Claire Cross
US Editor Kayla Dugger
US Executive Editor Lori Hand
Project Designer Vanessa Hamilton
Senior Designer Barbara Zuniga
Managing Editor Dawn Henderson
Managing Art Editor Marianne Markham
Senior Production Editor Tony Phipps
Senior Jacket Designer Nicola Powling
Jacket Coordinator Lucy Philpott
Art Director Maxine Pedliham
Publishing Director Katie Cowan

Illustrator Yeji Kim

First American Edition, 2021
Published in the United States by DK Publishing
1745 Broadway, 20th Floor, New York, NY 10019

Copyright © 2021 Dorling Kindersley Limited
DK, a Division of Penguin Random House LLC
23 24 25 10 9 8 7 6 5 4 3
008–322814–Aug/2021

A catalog record for this book
is available from the Library of Congress.
ISBN 978-0-7440-3374-8

DK books are available at special discounts when purchased
in bulk for sales promotions, premiums, fund-raising,
or educational use. For details, contact: DK Publishing
Special Markets,
1745 Broadway, 20th Floor, New York, NY 10019
SpecialSales@dk.com

Printed and bound in China

For the curious
www.dk.com

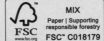

MIX
Paper | Supporting
responsible forestry
FSC™ C018179

This book was made with Forest
Stewardship Council™ certified
paper – one small step in DK's
commitment to a sustainable future.
**For more information go to
www.dk.com/our-green-pledge**